The Dale Car

**Effective Speaking,
Personality Development,
and the Art of
How to Win Friends & Influence People**

Dale Carnegie

SCHEDULE OF SESSIONS
Dale Carnegie Course

Effective Speaking, Personality Development and
The Art of Winning Friends and Influencing People

The Dale Carnegie Course is presented in New York
by the Institute of Effective Speaking and Personality
Development—Dale Carnegie, President. Chartered
by the Board of Regents of the University of the State
of New York (New York State Department of Education).

TABLE OF CONTENTS

6:00 to 8:00 P.M. SESSIONS

TABLE OF CONTENTS

8:00 to 10:40 P.M. SESSIONS

HOW TO GET THE MOST OUT OF THIS COURSE

by DALE CARNEGIE

You, as a student of this course, are setting out on a bold and worthy enterprise.

At the termination of this training, you will probably be astonished at how much you have gained from it. You will probably have progressed far more than you now dream possible. For the rest of your life, you may look back upon this course as the turning point of your career. These statements sound like wild exaggerations, don't they? But they are not. They are the sober truth. I know, because I have seen this training, for over a third of a century, work miracles in the lives of men and women.

We Help You to Help Yourself

However, what you get out of this training will depend largely on the fire of your inner urge. All we can do is to help you help yourself. That is all Princeton, McGill, Yale or Harvard could do for you. In fact, Dr. A. Lawrence Lowell, a former president of Harvard, said, "There is only one thing which will really train the human mind, and that is the voluntary use of the mind by the man himself. You may aid him. You may guide him. You may suggest to him; and, above all else, you may inspire him; but the only thing worth having is that which he gets by his own exertions; and what he gets is in direct proportion to what he puts into it."

Your Attitude Is Important

Sometimes men and women enroll for this course with a lackadaisical attitude, saying, "Here is my enrollment fee. Now let's see what you can do for me."

4

If that is your attitude, we beg you not to take the course because we can't do much for you.

On the other hand, if you say, "I am giving you my enrollment fee; and, in addition, I am going to give you my enthusiastic cooperation; I believe in this training and I am going after it like a bulldog after a cat"—if that is your attitude, we can help you help yourself to an extent that will almost take your breath away.

One of the most valuable qualities you will develop in this course is the ability to speak with more poise, more courage and more self-confidence, regardless of whether you are talking to one person or a thousand.

I have written a book entitled "How to Stop Worrying and Start Living." I have read almost every book written in English on that subject. I have discussed it with thousands of people. I have been training men to develop courage and self-confidence for more than thirty years. Now I can honestly say that if there has ever been devised a better way of conquering fear and developing courage than the training you will receive in this course, I have never heard of it.

Think Yourself Brave and You Will Be

You have already begun to conquer fear. You have already taken a bold and courageous step by enrolling for this course. I want you to begin right this instant to think of yourself as a person of courage, for, as you think, so you will be. Who is stopping you from being self-confident and self-reliant right now? I am not stopping you. Neither is the person sitting next to you. Nobody is stopping you but you, yourself.

Having courage does not depend on what is happening outside you. It depends on what is happening inside you. Only thoughts can give you courage and

5

only thoughts can give you fear. So start right now thinking thoughts of courage.

This Supervised Practice Will Help You

Use every opportunity you have in this course to practice speaking. Attend the 6:00 to 8:00 p.m. sessions, the 8:00 to 10:40 p.m. sessions and the drill-in-speaking sessions. George Bernard Shaw told me that years ago, when he was a young man eager to conquer shyness and timidity and his fear of speaking in public, he attended every meeting in London where there was to be a public discussion and always arose and took part in the debate. He got so excited about Socialism that he spent almost every other night, for twelve years, preaching Socialism on street corners, debating with hecklers and addressing audiences in halls and churches all over England and Scotland. Finally, this young man, who had been too shy and timid to ring the doorbell of his close friends, made himself one of the most brilliant speakers and debaters of his age.

Take a tip from George Bernard Shaw. Speak at every opportunity. Become interested in the activities of your community, your business or profession. Join the Red Cross and community club drives or the Little Theatre. Take an active part in politics and in talks and discussions everywhere.

Get Busy and Fear Will Vanish

Afraid? Go right on in spite of your fear—and fear will vanish. That is the advice that was given me by General A. A. Vandergrift, head of the United States Marine Corps. I asked him if soldiers were afraid going into battle with shells bursting all around them. He replied, "Any man who says he isn't afraid under those conditions is either lying or he has a weak mind; but the thing to do is to go right on and get busy and ignore your fears and they will vanish." General Vandergrift told me that his favorite motto is: "God favors the bold and strong of heart."

HOW THIS COURSE IS CONDUCTED

Your class meets two evenings a week. On one of these evenings, the session is divided into two parts, a first part which begins at 6:00 o'clock and a second part which begins at 8:00 o'clock. The session ends at 10:40. (In some cities, this session is held in the private dining room of a club, restaurant or hotel. The first part is conducted while dinner is in progress.) The other session, known as the drill-in-speaking session, usually runs from 7:00 to 10:30 p.m. As every student speaks one or more times at each session, you have the opportunity to make, during the course, a total of from 60 to 100 speeches. Because you have so many chances to speak and because of the helpful suggestions you receive from your instructors, you make rapid progress in building ease, poise and self-confidence—you learn to speak by speaking. (If you are compelled to miss any sessions, you may make them up in future classes without any additional cost.)·

You will be given three textbooks and several booklets to read and study. You will not be quizzed or examined on these books.

The first three sessions of the course are designed to give you ease on the platform and to help you develop confidence in speaking. The next two sessions give you practice in speaking. Sessions Six and Seven give you the magic formula for a speech. The remaining sessions teach you to use the newly acquired techniques in all kinds of speech situations.

7

Your Instructors Are Especially Trained

The Carnegie instructors are men who have been trained by Dale Carnegie or his associate, Percy H. Whiting, sometimes assisted by outstanding senior members of the faculty.

The instructors come from speech departments and English departments of leading universities, from executive and managerial positions in the business world, from the pulpit, from the lecture platform and from other professional positions. They are permitted to teach the Dale Carnegie Course only when they have proved, after a series of demonstrations, that they have the ability to help you to achieve the utmost in this course.

The instructors conduct the second part of the two-part session. They tell you what is right with your talk and what is wrong with it, and how to remedy and to improve it. They may tell you how to earn the right to make a speech, how to make your talk interesting, how to give it audience impact; they may put you through a series of drills to help you learn the use of the "Magic Formula" or to improve your delivery. They will also help you to solve your human relations problems.

The Job of the Class Directors Is to Help You

The class directors are outstanding graduates of the course who have been selected by their class members and the sponsor for this honor. They have been especially trained in a directors school. They are taught to be of service to you as you take each step forward in this self-improvement course.

The class directors conduct the drill-in-speaking sessions and the first part of the two-part sessions. These men are here to guide and inspire you and to help you overcome fear, to become more effective speakers and to apply the rules for winning friends and influencing people. They are available to counsel with you as friends, to help you over the rough spots and to bring you through the course triumphantly to the end.

Prizes Awarded at Most Sessions

In a few sessions, books are awarded as prizes, but in most of the other sessions, three mechanical pencils are offered. The green pencil, for the best speech, and the red pencil, for most improvement, are awarded on a secret vote of the class. The black pencil, the special award for achievement, is awarded by the class directors, after consultation with the instructor. No student is eligible to win more than one green pencil, one red pencil and one black pencil.

Please Bring Your Red Book to Each Session

You will find, in the following pages, a description of all sessions. These sessions will be taught, as a rule, in the order in which they appear in this book.

At the end of each session in this book, you will find a brief summary of the talks you will be required to make each evening, a list of the prizes which will be awarded and your reading assignment for that session.

Please bring this book with you to all sessions.

HOW YOU WILL BE TRAINED IN THIS COURSE

by DALE CARNEGIE

We have tried to select as instructors for this course men with sparkle and enthusiasm—men with a purpose, men with a sense of mission, men with a passionate desire to serve you.

Carnegie instructors have been especially trained in the basic philosophy of our instruction. All instructors and class directors have been provided with a book entitled "How to Teach the Dale Carnegie Course." They have also been provided with books containing complete directions for handling each session. So, regardless of whether you are taking this course in Boston, Winnipeg or Los Angeles, you should be getting substantially the same course that is given in New York.

Instructors will train you according to the basic philosophy of this course as outlined in the booklet entitled "A Quick and Easy Way to Learn to Speak in Public."

Instructors will train and teach you strictly according to the assignments in *The Little Red Book*. So, to get the greatest value possible from each session, be sure to read each assignment in the **Red Book** carefully and prepare accordingly.

How Carnegie Instructors Will Train You

You can depend on it that:

1. Your instructor will *NOT* deliver lectures. Ours is *not* a lecture course. It is a *drill* course. It is a course in which you do the speaking and the instructor helps you to speak more effectively.

10

2. Your instructor will not, as a rule, talk for more than three minutes at the opening of a session.

3. Your instructor will comment on each talk immediately after it is completed.

4. Your instructor will begin each session promptly at 8:00 p.m. and close promptly at 10:40 p.m.

5. Unless he is obliged to catch a train, your instructor will remain after class for consultation with anyone who desires additional help.

6. Your instructor will never make his comments all criticism. He will tell you what is *right,* as well as what is *wrong,* with your talks.

7. Your instructor will not merely tell you that your talk is *good.* He will also point out to you, and the class, *why it is good.* For example, he may say that it was good because it had one single idea backed up with a good illustration and that you spoke with sincerity and animation.

You Will Learn How to Improve Your Talk

8. When telling you what is wrong with your talk, your instructor will also tell you *how* it could be improved. To illustrate what I have in mind, an instructor in commenting on a talk that was not clear, might say something like this: "I liked your story and I admired your sincerity and the feeling you put into your talk. Your delivery was excellent, but the point of your talk wasn't quite clear to me. Won't you please state, in one sentence, the point you were trying to make?" After you have stated the point, he might say, "Fine! Splendid! Always make your point so clear that a weak-minded individual would understand it."

9. Your instructor will not, as a regular practice, tell you what is wrong with your talk without asking

11

you to do part of it over again. If, for example, you are lacking in animation, he will pick a few sentences out of your talk and ask you to say them over again with more spirit. He will keep you repeating these until you speak with adequate life and feeling. In this way, you will achieve a successful performance and learn by doing.

10. Your instructor will never criticize harshly. He will tell you gently, tactfully and kindly how to improve your performance and he will do it with a sincere desire to help.

11. If your instructor feels that he can help you improve your English, your grammar or your appearance, he will not embarrass you by calling your attention to these imperfections before the class. Instead, he will talk to you privately after the close of the session.

12. If you stand in a slouchy, "don't-care" attitude, nothing will be said about it in the first three sessions. After the third session, however, your instructor may urge you to stand up tall and act as if you were alive. Why? Because, if a man forces himself to act enthusiastically, he will tend to speak enthusiastically.

Never Memorize a Talk

13. Your instructor will urge you to refrain from writing out and memorizing your talks for three reasons:

a. Such talks invariably sound "written." They sound like a speech instead of something that comes from the heart.

b. You may forget your memorized words. (If you do, your audience will probably be glad you did—since no one wants to listen to memorized words.)

c. The man who is delivering a memorized speech rarely talks to his listeners. He has, instead, a faraway look in his eyes and a faraway sound in his voice.

14. Your instructor will set an example of animation and earnestness.

15. Your instructor will continually give encouragement to you and to other students.

16. This, above all: your instructor will, in dealings with the class, constantly practice and teach the rules in *How to Win Friends and Influence People*.

Qualities we hope to have in all our instructors are infinite kindness, patience and a passion to serve students. It was said of Confucius: "He never tried to impress his listeners with his exclusive knowledge. Instead, he tried to enlighten them with his inclusive sympathy." We have tried to instill this quality in our instructors.

Carnegie Instructors Will Get Down to Basic Fundamentals

Your instructor will train you in such basic fundamentals as:

1. Adequate preparation—choosing the right subject for you—talking on subjects you have earned the right to talk about—being interested in your subject.

2. Speaking with spirit and animation.

3. Having a good time speaking.

4. Having a natural, conversational opening. To find out whether you have a good opening, imagine yourself saying it across the dinner table to a friend.

5. Having a mental and emotional impact on the audience. Your speech will be judged by your instructor largely on the answers to these questions:

    a. Did it interest your listeners?

    b. Instruct them?

    c. Help them?

    d. Inspire them?

    e. Impress them?

    f. Move them to act?

If the answers are "yes," it was a good speech—regardless of how many small faults it had. If it didn't do anything to the listeners, it was a failure—regardless of how many virtues it had.

Carnegie Instructors Will Not Teach You Comparatively Unimportant Things

If this course ran for four years, we might try to improve your voice, your breathing, your vocabulary. This course lasts, however, not four years, but four months. So we stick to fundamentals. We do not try to teach:

1. *Voice*—You are probably not aspiring to become an actor or a professional public speaker so your voice is no doubt quite adequate for ordinary purposes. If you were given voice exercises, two things would happen. First, in order to achieve an improvement in the quality of your voice, you would probably have to practice boring voice exercises an hour or two a day for a year or more. Second, voice training would make you self-conscious. We help you to build self-confidence, not self-consciousness.

If you make an interesting talk, your listeners will not be any more conscious of your voice than they are of the air they are breathing. Though Lincoln and Theodore Roosevelt had high, thin, tenor voices, nobody cared, because they had something to say that was worth listening to. H. G. Wells had a voice that was so high-pitched it was almost feminine; yet he was paid a thousand dollars a night for speaking.

2. *Foreign Accents*—If a speaker with a foreign accent can be easily understood, your instructor will not attempt to correct his accent. Don't worry about an accent. A slight accent is often an asset. It frequently gives distinction to a man and charm to a woman. Your audience would a thousand times rather listen to an interesting speaker with an accent than to a dull speaker who spoke the king's English with immaculate precision.

15

Just Go Ahead and Breathe!

3. *Breathing*—You have been getting along pretty well all your life without thinking of breathing. Why harass yourself by thinking about it now when you ought to be concentrating on your message and your listeners? Forget it.

4. *Eye-Contact*—(Looking at your audience.) If you don't have good eye-contact, your instructor won't say a word about it in the early sessions of the course. Why? Because calling your attention to it would—

    a. Increase your self-consciousness.

    b. Get your mind off your talk.

If you don't look straight at your listeners, your instructor will, in later sessions, remedy that by dealing with the causes that produce it. How? By encouraging you to talk about something that you know and feel and desire to communicate to your audience. If you have something to say that interests you, something that you want to get over to your audience, you can't keep from looking the audience straight in the eye. When a cat is getting ready to spring on a mouse, she never has any trouble with eye-contact. And neither do you have any trouble with eye-contact when you are having a hot argument at home or in the office.

5. *"Word Whiskers"*—During the early part of the course, your instructor won't call your attention to the "uhs" and "ahs" and "umms" that we call "word whiskers." Instead, your instructor will help you get rid of word whiskers by encouraging you to talk *about something you know well and feel and are eager to communicate to your audience.* A few word whiskers aren't serious. I have heard Winston Churchill use word whiskers. It is possible to make a superb talk and

16

still have word whiskers. *It isn't faults that kill a talk, it is a lack of virtues.*

However, if you have developed the bad habit of repeatedly saying, "Ah" and "Er," your instructor will call your attention to this habit in the last half of the course—after you have gained confidence and ease in speaking.

Smile if You Want To

6. *Smiling*—Your instructor will not urge you to smile unless a smile would naturally fit you and your subject. If you are talking about the enjoyment you are getting out of this course, you would naturally smile; but if you were speaking about having rheumatic fever, you would hardly smile. Franklin D. Roosevelt often smiled as he talked. It was natural for him to do so. It wasn't natural for Calvin Coolidge to smile. Be yourself. Don't try to imitate others.

7. *Hands in Pockets* — In the early part of the course, your instructor will not criticize you for keeping your hands in your pockets. Why? Because calling your attention to such unimportant details at that time would only confuse you and make you self-conscious. It would cause you to take your mind off your talk and get you thinking about trivial details that are relatively unimportant. When a speaker is half-blinded with fear, he ought to do anything within reason that makes him feel more comfortable. If he is terrified, keeping his hands in his pockets may make him feel more comfortable. Who cares anyway what he does with his hands? We are interested only in what he can do to us. If he can entertain, inspire or help us solve our problems, we won't notice or care whether his hands are in his pockets or behind his back or in his hair. I have seen William Jennings Bryan and Theodore Roosevelt

17

—two of the most eloquent speakers in American political history—speak with their hands in their pockets.

However, during the last half of the course, after you have gained ease and confidence, your instructor will urge you to keep your hands out of your pockets because you are more likely to gesture when your hands are hanging free at your sides. And gesturing is important—if it comes naturally to you—because it helps you to relax and let go and speak more naturally.

Some Gesture—Some Don't

8. *Gestures*—When you are self-conscious, during the first few sessions of the course, your instructor will not urge you to gesture. However, if you do make gestures naturally, he will praise you and encourage you to keep on using gestures.

Your instructor will not give you any rules for gesturing. You will not be taught that certain positions of the hand mean this or that. You will not be told to lift your arms and gesture from the shoulder. You will not be told to use the right hand or the left hand; but you will be urged to make any movements that come naturally to you. If your gestures come as a result of an inner urge to get your message across, you won't be conscious that you are gesturing, and neither will your listeners.

The kind and amount of gestures that you make will depend on your temperament. Theodore Roosevelt gestured almost constantly with his hands and his fists. Franklin D. Roosevelt gestured by movements of his head. On the other hand, Calvin Coolidge rarely gestured, and neither did Herbert Hoover. Gestures didn't fit their personalities. As far as gestures are concerned, you should do what comes naturally to you. However, if you possibly can, use gestures—any gestures that come naturally—because they will help you to put more life and warmth and color into your speaking.

9. *Vocabulary*—Your instructor will assure you that you don't need a large vocabulary to be a good speaker. Even if you knew the dictionary by heart, we would urge you to use the simple, everyday language that Lincoln used—words that even a child can understand.

Education Doesn't Make the Speaker

10. *College Education*—Your instructor will assure you that your ability to speak effectively depends very little on how many years you spent in school. I once had in the same class two men with sharply different backgrounds. One had formerly been an instructor in Harvard. The other man had, as a boy, run away to sea. Years later, his wife had taught him to read. This sailor made better talks than the erstwhile Harvard instructor. Why? Because he had a better personality, more sparkle, more enthusiasm, more experience, more to talk about.

A college education may improve your ability to speak—or it may not. The only kind of education that counts is self-education. That is the kind Edison had —he attended school only six weeks. That is the kind Ben Franklin had—he attended school less than a year. That is the kind Lincoln had—he attended school only six months, yet he delivered two of the most famous speeches ever delivered by mortal man. Your instructor will assure you that your progress in this course will depend far more on your determination to learn than upon a college education. So don't develop an inferiority complex because of your lack of formal education.

Does this mean that I feel that a college education is not worth while? No. It is highly desirable for some men. It is not worth while for others. Speaking for myself, I am glad I spent four years in college. If I hadn't done so, I would now probably be plowing corn on a Missouri farm.

What You Will Be Taught to Do

Your instructor will urge you to:

1. Concentrate on your message and on your listeners instead of thinking of yourself.

2. Let yourself go before an audience just as you do in spirited conversation at home or in business.

3. Be yourself.

4. Have a good time speaking. Your attitude is as contagious as the measles. If you have a good time talking to us, the chances are we will have a good time listening to you.

5. Get on "top of your talk" instead of letting your talk get on "top of you." (This can be done by talking about something that you have earned the right to talk about—something you know and feel and are eager to tell us about.)

6. Think of yourself as a Western Union boy delivering a telegram. No one cares what the messenger boy looks like or how he stands or what he does. We are interested only in what the telegram says. An audience is like that too. Have a telegram—a message that is worthy of their attention.

7. Be clear.

8. Be impressive and convincing.

9. Be interesting.

10. Begin your talk in an interesting, conversational manner.

11. Have a good closing.

12. Illustrate your points with a concrete case or example.

13. Speak with contagious enthusiasm.

14. Throw yourself and your personality into your talk.

15. Realize how easy it is to speak in public when you follow the suggestions in the booklet, *A Quick and Easy Way to Learn to Speak in Public.*

Getting Acquainted ....6:00 to 8:00 p.m.

Overcoming Fear ....8:00 to 10:40 p.m.

Date..

Instructor..

Getting Acquainted—6:00 to 8:00 p.m.

The first part of the session tonight will provide you with an opportunity to get acquainted with the other members of your class.

One of the best ways to get acquainted is to learn nicknames. In order to give you both an incentive and an opportunity to learn the nicknames of all class members, a "Nickname" Contest will be staged tonight. Here is how it is done:

1. The first speaker will stand and give his name and nickname. (Please do it slowly, loudly and distinctly.) SPELL both your name and your nickname. Then tell us how to remember the name and nickname. Next, Number 2 will give his name and nickname, and so on through the group.

2. As each class member states his nickname, you should try to etch it on your memory. If the class is not too large, you will be asked to remember both the surname and the nickname.

3. Each man* will then be called—by his surname and his nickname—for a brief talk. He should tell us why he is taking the course and what he hopes to get out of it.

---

*Throughout this book, we say, "the man," "the men," and "he will." Quite obviously, in almost every case, we mean "the man or woman," "the men and women," and "he or she will."

4. After the talks, the director will ask each man to rise—first Number 1, then Number 2, and so on. Each speaker, as soon as he rises, will call his *number* in a loud voice, and will stand and look at the class for 12 seconds—long enough to give everyone an opportunity to write his nickname on a sheet provided for the purpose. For example, Number 1, "Jim," Number 2, "Bill," etc.

5. Next, you will pass your paper to the person on your right.

6. The director will then call the numbers. As a student's name is called, he will stand and again state his name and nickname. Each person will correct the paper he holds.

7. The director will then call for the totals to determine who remembered the most nicknames and will present a special award for achievement to the memory champion of the class.

Visitors Are Welcome at This Session

Haven't you a friend, employee, associate or even a "boss" who could also profit by this training? If so, why not bring him as your guest? He will be most welcome.

Visitors are always welcome at the first and second sessions, the election session and the graduation session. They are permitted to attend any other session provided they are invited by a student, with the approval of the class director or of a sponsor.

Drill-in-Speaking Sessions Begin This Week

You will start your drill-in-speaking sessions this week and will continue them once a week throughout the course. These sessions will help you get the greatest possible benefit out of this course.

Overcoming Fear—8:00 to 10:40 p.m.

You will be requested in this second part of the first session to talk for not over two minutes about yourself. That ought to be easy, very easy, because you are the world's best authority on that subject.

Don't try to make a speech—just answer the questions listed below. You won't have to stand when you talk. You and several other students will be called to the front of the room at the same time and will sit together on a table facing the class. Relax and talk about your experiences. It will be thrilling. After you get started, you will almost enjoy it.

You will discover how easy it is to talk when you have something to say that you want to say—something that you know thoroughly. Your talk should be an answer to several of the questions given on this page and on page 25. Please be sure to answer questions 1, 2, 3, 4 and 9. If you wish, you may hold this booklet in your hand and read the questions before you answer them.

Here Are the Questions

1. What is your name? Enunciate your name very clearly. If it is at all unusual, spell it.

2. Where do you live?

3. Where do you work?

4. What kind of work do you do?

5. Was this course recommended to you?

If so, by whom? Did he say how he had profited by this training? Why did he urge you to take it?

24

6. If you did not learn about this course through a former student, how did you learn about it?

Did you receive a letter about it? Did you read any newspaper advertisements? When you read the advertisement, did you say, "Here is just the thing I've been looking for," or were you a bit skeptical? Did you discuss it with friends? What did they say about the course? Why did you attend the first meeting?

7. If you heard former students speak at the opening session, what did you think of their talks?

Were you surprised at the stories they related? What effect did their talks have on you? Which of the speakers impressed you most? Why?

8. Did you ever try to talk in public before?

If so, when, where, why? What happened? How did you feel? Be specific. Give dates, names, places and interesting details.

9. What do you hope to get out of this training?

Tell us about your speaking problems or your human relations problems. Tell us why you are joining this course.

10. How do you expect to use this training in your business or profession?

11. Do you want to be able to think on your feet and to express yourself before groups? Why? Where? How will it help you?

12. Do you want to learn more about how to win friends and influence people? Why? In what ways do you fail in human relations? Give examples. Be definite. Be specific. Tell us what you have observed.

If you prefer to talk about something else, do so. You are at liberty in every session of this course to talk on any subject you choose.

A mechanical pencil inscribed "First Prize for Best Speech, Dale Carnegie Course in Effective Speaking" will be awarded by a vote of the class for the best talk.

All Students Are Allowed Equal Speaking Time

All speeches in this course, unless otherwise specified, are limited to two minutes. Your director will start a stop watch with the first word of your talk. If you are still speaking at the end of the allotted time, he will ring a bell. He is under strict orders not to wait for a pause in your speech or for the end of a sentence. No—he must ring the bell on the exact second when your talking time expires.

If you are at the end of a sentence when the bell rings, you should stop instantly. If, however, you are in the middle of a sentence when the bell rings, you should finish that sentence, provided you can do it in 20 seconds or less.

To sum it up:

1. When the bell rings, finish the sentence you have started.

2. After the bell rings—

   a. Do not drag the sentence out more than 20 seconds.

   b. Do not start a new sentence.

This rule is in force because it would be a discourtesy to the class if one student tried to talk longer than the rest, and because it would not be fair to allow one student to take more time than the others.

You Will Not Be Criticized
in the Early Sessions

Certain ambitious, impatient students in every class feel they should be told, at the outset of the course, all about their faults. We tried this system and discarded it decades ago. We discovered that criticism in the first few sessions does far more harm than good. Sometimes it is disastrous. For example, suppose you tell a nervous, excited individual, a man half-blinded with fear, that he didn't half open his mouth, that he couldn't be heard in the back of the room, that he said "jist," that he failed to make his point, that he lacked enthusiasm. Suppose you told him all that, what would happen? Would that build confidence? Would that help him in his battle to conquer fear and to think on his feet?

We know, from over a third of a century of experience, that at least fifty per cent of the faults you have now will disappear automatically as you develop courage and confidence. That is the first thing you need: *confidence*. The whole purpose of these first few sessions is to eliminate nervousness and to develop ease and poise.

Practice Will Cure Many Faults

A beginner should not be constantly reminded of a few superficial faults. He needs to be told the truth, namely: that he can and will, with practice, achieve results that now seem impossible.

Be patient. This training has been carefully planned. You will, at the proper time, have your attention called to your faults. A man does not expect to ride a bicycle on a tight rope until he has learned to balance himself on the ground. Don't expect all criticism and all ad-

27

vancement in one session. Effective speakers aren't built in a day.

Be reasonable about measuring your progress. Don't compare yourself with the best speakers in the class—unless you are *one* of them. Compare yourself, as the course progresses, with *yourself at the start*.

Your instructor will try to make each comment helpful, not only to the person who has just spoken, but also to everyone present. You will learn, not only from the comments on your own speeches, but quite as much from the comments on the speeches of other students. You will learn how to avoid the faults of others and how to acquire their good characteristics.

Suggestions That Will Help You Get the Most Out of This Course

Three groups of people will work with you during this course to help you to develop courage and confidence, the ability to think on your feet, the ability to speak before groups, and the ability to get along with others.

1. The class directors will help you in the first part of every two-part session, in drill-in-speaking sessions and in personal conferences.

2. The instructor will help you in the second part of every two-part session.

3. The members of your class will, in later sessions, be of great help to you in calling attention to your speaking faults.

In addition, you will be at work upon yourself.

Class directors, students and instructors can only encourage and guide you. Every change made in you

28

and every one of your achievements will depend upon what you do for yourself. Although others can give you advice, the development of your personality depends upon you. Your instructor or your class members can tell you, for example, to "be more animated," but only *you* can force yourself to display animation.

Do You Want to Enlarge Your Vocabulary?

Below are some practical suggestions for enlarging and enriching your vocabulary so that you may express your thoughts with more clarity, with more precision and in a more interesting way. Remember to keep your language simple—words are not used to astound the audience, or to impress them with your superior vocabulary—words are the tools of successful speaking. They are the transmitting device for your thoughts and ideas.

These Rules Really Work

Here are rules for acquiring a larger vocabulary:

1. Read well-written newspaper columns, good books, editorials and the works of the best magazine writers. Look up all unfamiliar words in the dictionary.

2. Listen to the better radio commentators and other trained speakers and note their choice of words. Compare their pronunciation and usage of words with yours. If your pronunciation and your understanding of the meaning of a word differ from theirs, refer to your dictionary for the correct pronunciation and meaning.

3. Read aloud from well-written books.

4. Provide yourself with a good dictionary and a good thesaurus and use them.

5. Study lists of words and their correct usage. You will find such lists in your textbook, *Public Speaking and Influencing Men in Business,* at the end of each chapter under the section headed "Speech Building."

6. Have your wife, friends and children correct you when you misuse words. Look up their correct meaning, usage and pronunciation in your dictionary—and thereafter use them correctly.

7. Learn one new word a day. Not only look up meanings and accents, but use the word in sentences. If you get in the habit of doing this daily, you will find your vocabulary increased by 365 new words each year!

Talks, Prizes and Reading Assignment
Session Number One

Talks:

6:00 to 8:00 p.m. session—Nickname Contest.

8:00 to 10:40 p.m. session—You answer a few questions about yourself.

Prizes:

6:00 to 8:00 p.m. session—Special award pencil to the Nickname Champion.

8:00 to 10:40 p.m. session—Best speech pencil.

Reading Assignment:

No reading assignment.

How to Answer Questions—6:00 to 8:00 p.m.

Before you start your talks tonight, you will say that justly famous poem:

> Mary had a little lamb,
> Its fleece was white as snow,
> And everywhere that Mary went
> The lamb was sure to go.

No—it's not elocution—it's a "warm up." We want to get you out of your shell and to encourage you to gesture. This is how it will be done. Groups of eight or ten students will be brought to the front of the room and will recite in unison the above poem in these four ways: (1) in a whisper, (2) with laughter, (3) with sadness, (4) with anger. As soon as each group has finished, the class will vote by a show of hands as to who did the best job. The group winners will then be matched in the final round for the class championship. In this last round they will say the verse in these four ways: (1) in pantomime, (2) very dramatic, (3) dead pan and frozen solid, (4) with super-animation.

Tonight You Just Answer Questions

Good news for you tonight. You needn't give a thought to what you are going to say at this session.

31

All you have to do is answer questions! When your turn comes, please stand up and start by answering the question, "What do you do for a living?"

Perhaps you can talk for your allotted time (90 seconds) on the subject. If you can't, your class members will ask you questions—such questions as: "What do you do as an electrical engineer?" . . . "What is there about your work that is interesting?" . . . "How did you come to get into that line of work?" . . . "How long do you have to study to be an electrical engineer?" . . . "Is the field overcrowded?" . . . "What concern do you work for?" . . . "What are your problems?"

If you are unable to answer certain questions, don't be embarrassed—admit that you can't answer them and let it go at that.

Your directors will keep this question-asking period moving. If it begins to drag, they will ask questions themselves or will call certain students by name, and request them to ask questions.

This question—"How did you come to get into your line of work?"—is one that almost everyone likes to answer. Be sure to ask that question of every member of the class tonight who finds trouble in talking for his full 90 seconds.

This question-answering experience will demonstrate to you how easy it is for you to face an audience and think and talk on your feet when you know precisely what you are talking about. This experience will help you develop ease and self-confidence. It will also help the class members to become better acquainted with one another.

Developing Courage—8:00 to 10:40 p.m.

You will make the best talks about those things which you have experienced—have lived. You can talk most easily about your own life. You know that subject. You *know* that you know it. So you will talk tonight on "An Interesting Event in My Life."

Don't recite a few bare, colorless facts—don't try to tell us the whole story of your life. Instead, give us in detail *one single interesting event.*

What a Naval Lieutenant Said

For example, Lt. (jg) Alton J. Childers, U. S. Naval Reserve, made this talk:

"I was on a merchant ship in charge of the naval armed guard crew when in September, 1942, she was twice hit amidships by torpedoes and sent to the bottom of the South Atlantic off South America. I had to swim in shark-infested waters for about 45 minutes before I was rescued by a British ship. That experience held no more terror for me than the ordeal of talking before a strange group of people.

"It is in order to get over that fear that I am taking the Dale Carnegie Course. If it will do that for me— if it will also enable me to organize my thoughts effectively and to express them with some degree of conviction, it will prove the most profitable investment I ever made. (P.S. It did!)"

This was a good talk because it was narrowed down to one point and contained one interesting incident. Maybe you haven't been torpedoed, but certainly you can give one single interesting event in your life. If it is interesting to you, it is likely to be interesting to your audience.

33

Try Some of These Subjects

We suggest that you answer some of these questions:

Where were you born? What is the first incident in your life that you can remember? What were your childhood ambitions? Did you go to college? If so, why? Has it paid? How? If you did not go to college, why not, and do you regret not having gone? Why?

How did you earn your first dollar? How did you get your first job?

What is the most exciting thing that ever happened to you? Tell us that. Or what was your narrowest escape?

What great mistake have you made in your life, that you wouldn't make if you had your life to live over? Tell us about that.

Or tell us the most embarrassing thing that ever happened to you. Or the funniest.

People are always interested in a struggle, so tell us about your struggles to get ahead, your failures, your achievements, your joys or your sorrows.

Look back over your life and pick out an incident that stirred your feelings and aroused your emotions. That will be easy to talk about. What was it: Death? Financial disaster? Poverty? The battle to establish a business of your own?

Or perhaps you prefer one of these subjects: "The most interesting trip I ever made," "The most interesting thing I ever did in my life," "If I had to move to another country, I would choose . . . because . . . ."

34

Try It Out on Your Friends

Select at once the incident you are going to talk about and discuss it with your friends at every opportunity this week.

The fact that you have talked this event over informally will be helpful when you stand up to speak.

To repeat, don't try to cover the whole story of your life. *Talk about only one interesting incident.* This talk, and all talks in this course, unless otherwise specified, will be limited to two minutes.

Under no circumstances should you write out what you are going to say or try to memorize it word for word. That almost always proves to be disastrous. Don't even think of "making a speech." Merely stand up and chat with us about your experiences in the same spontaneous, casual way you would talk to a person across the dinner table.

You will find a table on the platform tonight. You can sit on it, lean against it or disregard it—just as you please.

Visitors Are Welcome at This Session

Surely you have a friend, a customer, or a business associate who would be interested in this training. If so, why not bring him with you as your guest tonight, to both sessions? We feel sure he will find the evening highly entertaining.

A Little Study Will Pay Big Dividends

Be sure to read the sections assigned in the textbooks. They are interesting; they are easy to read; they are most helpful. If you go over this assigned reading carefully each week, you will get vastly more out of the course. It will take a little time—it will pay big dividends.

Tonight You Get the Secret of Successful Speaking

You will receive tonight a booklet by Dale Carnegie entitled "A Quick and Easy Way to Learn to Speak in Public." This booklet reveals the secrets of effective speaking that it took Dale Carnegie over thirty years to discover. These secrets have never before been told so clearly and illustrated so vividly. We urge you to carry this booklet with you and to read it at least three times this week. Read it; study it; underscore it; and make it your guide-book in this course.

Suggestions About All Sessions

Keep a Record of the Comments on Your Talks

We suggest that you keep a written record of every comment, good or bad, made by instructors, class directors, or your fellow students on your talks, throughout the course. One man became the best speaker in his class largely by constantly reviewing his notes and working on his weak points.

Don't Keep Changing Subjects

Here is a suggestion about selecting subjects for all sessions: Pick the subject you are going to talk about at the next session the day after the class meeting and *stick* to it. Don't change your subject again and again. If you do, you will never be prepared.

This Thought Will Encourage You

"I'm still a little frightened," you say.
That's nothing. Probably all your life you will be a

little *nervous* in the first minute or two of a speech. Virtually all good speakers are nervous at the start of a speech. Not afraid—their knees do not knock together or their teeth chatter, but their pulse is a little faster and they are on edge. Because they are on edge, they can make a better talk.

And so can you.

Experienced speakers find that, after they have been talking a minute or two, their nervousness disappears—and *so will yours.*

Remember that, in this course, you are giving the hard part of your speech—the first two minutes. You will find, in all your future speaking, your nervousness will disappear after the first minute or two and, from there on, you will talk quite as calmly and easily to a large audience as you would to a group of friends.

So our advice to you is: Don't worry over those first two minutes.

Basis on Which Diplomas Are Awarded

In order to obtain a diploma, you must: (a) be certified by your instructor (or instructors) and class directors as having made progress worthy of the award of a diploma and (b) have completed payment of your tuition.

Talks, Prizes and Reading Assignment
Session Number Two

Talks:

6:00 to 8:00 p.m. session—90 seconds—Talk about your business or profession or answer questions.

8:00 to 10:40 p.m. session—2 minutes—Talk on an interesting event in your life.

Prizes:

8:00 to 10:40 p.m. session—Best speech, most improvement and special award pencils.

Reading Assignment:

In preparation for Session No. 2, please read in the textbook, *Public Speaking and Influencing Men in Business:*

Chapter I—"Developing Courage and Self-Confidence"—Pages 3 through 28.

Please do not forget to read each week the section on "Speech Building" in each of the assigned chapters in *Public Speaking and Influencing Men in Business.*

At Session No. 1 you were given Dale Carnegie's latest book, *How to Stop Worrying and Start Living.*

Please begin reading this book now in preparation for your talk in Session No. 12—and begin putting the rules into practice. You will be assigned chapters to read in this book each week. This week please read pages 1 through 28.

SESSION No. 3

Acquiring Ease and
    Confidence ....6:00 to 8:00 p.m.
How to Make Rapid and Easy
    Progress in This Course......8:00 to 10:40 p.m.

Date..

Instructor..

Acquiring Ease and Confidence—
6:00 to 8:00 p.m.

Tonight, you will be given a drill in gestures. You ought to gesture occasionally when speaking, not because the gestures will affect the audience, but because they will affect you. They will make you loosen up and talk with more naturalness, more variety, more color, more emphasis. The moment you let yourself go physically, you will tend to let yourself go mentally and emotionally. Dale Carnegie declares he can shut his eyes and tell whether or not a speaker is gesturing. He can tell by the life and sparkle and emphasis that gestures produce. When Dale Carnegie speaks on the radio, he gestures almost constantly. So do many radio announcers. Listeners cannot see these gestures, but they can hear the effects of them.

You can make gestures with your hands, as Theodore Roosevelt did; or, you can make them by nodding your head, as Franklin D. Roosevelt did.

Gestures Should Make Themselves

Gestures shouldn't be something you make mechanically. They should come from the inside out. They should be an outward manifestation of an inward con-

39

dition. When an experienced speaker is making gestures, he is rarely conscious that he is doing it; and neither is his audience. You are not conscious of gesturing when you get into a hot argument, but you probably gesture superbly then.

Become intensely interested in what you are saying and your gestures will probably take care of themselves. Let me repeat, gestures should come naturally, spontaneously. *But if they don't, then, in class and drill sessions, force yourself to make them.* Force yourself to make them regardless of how awkward, self-conscious and ridiculous you feel. Keep on forcing yourself to gesture in your talks before the members of your class, and presently you will find yourself gesturing naturally, easily, unconsciously.

You Visit a Box Factory

Tonight, we are going to ask you to make some absurd gestures describing your visit to an imaginary box factory. True, no one in his right mind would make, in a normal speech, all the gestures you will be required to make in this exercise. It is merely a drill to force you to loosen up and let yourself go. Since you will be brought to the platform with five or six other students and asked to repeat, with appropriate gestures, the following sentences, please memorize them:

I found myself yesterday near a huge box factory, located on a high hill. Running all around this building was a picket fence about this high.

I walked up to the factory, threw open the door, walked in and found myself in a long hallway.

At the far end of the hallway was a spiral staircase. I walked up this spiral staircase, pushed open a sliding door and found myself in a big room, piled high with

40

boxes. There were big boxes, middle-sized boxes and very small boxes.

Suddenly, the boxes started to tumble down around my head! I woke with a start—yawned, stretched, and went back to sleep.

After each group has gone through this exercise, the class will vote as to which person in the group gave the best performance. When all members of the class have gone through this "warm up" once, the various group winners will be matched in a final round, for the class championship.

Talk About Your Daily Work or Your Hobby

After the close of the box-factory contest, you will talk for 60 seconds about something you know thoroughly: your work, your business, your profession, your hobby.

Please Bring an .Exhibit

If possible, use some kind of exhibit to illustrate your talk. Using exhibits will help you in four ways:

1. Handling exhibits before an audience will help you to relax. This will help you to get your mind off yourself and feel more at ease.

2. Exhibits will help you make your talks clear and vivid.

3. Exhibits will help you to get and hold attention. An exhibit of any kind is almost sure-fire, regardless of whether it is a photograph, a shirt, or a piece of plastic. Your listeners will look at almost anything you hold up for them to see.

4. Exhibits will help you to make your talk memorable.

41

Dale Carnegie still remembers the talks of one of his students 19 years ago—a student who used exhibits in every speech he made. The night he spoke on his hobby of collecting harmless snakes he brought three specimens to class in a sack. One got loose and wriggled around the room—no one who was there ever forgot that speech!

Sometimes students say, "Oh, no exhibit will fit my talk." If that is true, get a new subject. Perhaps the easiest way is to select some interesting exhibit and build your talk around that.

If possible, bring an exhibit that will illustrate or explain your work. If you are a stenographer or a book-keeper, you may have to use some ingenuity in finding a satisfactory exhibit; but if you manufacture soap or build bridges, you can bring either an exhibit or pictures to illustrate your talk. One student last season— a man who ran a linotype machine for a newspaper— brought slugs of type metal that he made with his machine and passed them around as exhibits.

Help Your Listeners Solve Their Problems

Please remember, when you are talking about your business or profession, that listeners are primarily interested in their own problems. So, if possible, use the knowledge that you have acquired in your business to help your listeners solve their problems. That is what Ralph Gretsch did, when he was a student of this course in 1932. Mr. Gretsch was president of the Ralph Gretsch Co., Inc., 1133 Broadway, New York, N. Y. His company manufactured moth balls. So, when he talked about his business, he did a wise thing: He began by talking immediately about the problems of his listeners. He said in his first sentence, "I manufacture moth balls; and I am going to tell you how to keep moths from ruining your clothes and rugs." That promise snared everyone's interest instantly.

Why don't you try this same technique tonight? If you are a dentist, give us a talk on how to care for our teeth so well that we will rarely have to go to the dentist. Do that, and your listeners will love you for it.

If you are an attorney, tell us what will happen to our families if we die without leaving a will, or tell us how to so handle our affairs that we won't need to see an attorney often.

If you sell insurance, tell us what frequently happens to insurance money left in one lump sum to a wife or child.

If you are an accountant, tell us the reasons why so many people fail in business.

Ask Yourself Questions—Then Answer Them

In preparing your talk for tonight, write down a list of questions that people might ask about your business. Then tear up the questions and answer them in your talk. Don't write out your talk.

Don't try to make a formal speech tonight. Instead, merely chat with us about your work. You know a hundred times as much about it as you can tell in 60 seconds; so you will discover this evening how easy it is to talk when you know what you are talking about. We don't care, at this session, whether your speech has a formal beginning or an ending. We don't care about your delivery. We don't care about anything tonight except helping you to prove to yourself that you can face an audience and think on your feet and keep going—and get a sort of terrified enjoyment out of it.

43

Committees Will Be Appointed

Tonight your class director will appoint temporary class officers: president, vice-president, secretary and treasurer. He will also appoint some, but not all, of the standing committees. The temporary class officers will serve either until your class elects permanent officers after the last session or they may be changed several times, at the discretion of your class directors.

How to Make Rapid and Easy Progress in This Course—8:00 to 10:40 p.m.

Last week you were given a booklet written by Dale Carnegie entitled "A Quick and Easy Way to Learn to Speak in Public."

After you have read this booklet, you will understand what we mean when we say, "Don't spend ten minutes or ten hours preparing for this speech. Spend ten *years!*" Or, to say the same thing in another way, talk about something you have *earned the right to talk about.*

If you can't quickly and easily select a speech subject which you have earned the right to talk about, go back and reread *A Quick and Easy Way to Learn to Speak in Public.* Then ask yourself:

1. *What do I know the most about?* Can I talk about my family—surely I know all about that. My business? My hobby? You have earned the right to talk on any of those subjects.

2. What has deeply stirred me? Some religious experience? Love? Death? An exciting incident? A narrow escape? The greatest regret of my life? (Surely you can talk on one of those subjects.)

3. What "makes me mad"? High taxes? Dis-

44

courtesy of clerks? Street sprinkling? The divorce question? Careless drivers? Singing commercials? (What a speech you can make on some subject that makes you boil with rage!)

Pick the kind of topic that Dale Carnegie recommends in his booklet and you can't possibly fail. Open your mouth and your talk will jump right out.

How Students Will Be Called Up

In most sessions, students are called to the front six or eight at a time. They sit in the first row, which is reserved for speakers, and are called to the platform from there. When a student finishes his talk, he resumes his seat *in the front row.*

Carry These Rules With You

You will be given tonight a card listing the rules taught in *How to Win Friends and Influence People.* (These rules are presented also on the last pages of this Red Book.) You are urged to carry this card with you all the time and to keep reviewing and applying these rules. This won't be an easy task because man is naturally selfish and because these rules teach unselfishness.

Start Now to Prepare for the 4th Session

Would you like to make a good talk at the fourth session? Here is a formula that has rarely failed:

1. Pick out one of the *Fundamental Techniques for Handling People* or one of the *Six Rules for Making People Like You* (see page 163). You will get quicker results out of a positive rule like "Give appreciation" than out of a negative rule like "Don't criticize." Select the rule you break most often. For example, if

you do not give people sincere appreciation when they deserve it, pick Fundamental Technique No. 2 as the one to work on.

2. Consciously, conscientiously, consistently, put that rule into practice—every time you get a chance every day.

3. At the fourth session tell the class what happened and have no doubt on this point: Something *will have* happened—something worth talking about!

Start Now to Use These Rules

In order to give you ample time to apply the rules in preparation for your human relations talk in Session No. 4, please read now in *How to Win Friends and Influence People:*

"The Fundamental Techniques in Handling People," pages 25 through 71.

"Six Ways to Make People Like You," pages 75 through 133.

Talks, Prizes and Reading Assignment
Session Number Three

Talks:

6:00 to 8:00 p.m. session—60 seconds—Talk about your work or your hobby.

8:00 to 10:40 p.m. session—2 minutes—Talk on any subject which you have earned the right to talk about.

Prizes:

8:00 to 10:40 p.m. session—Best speech, most improvement and special award pencils.

46

Reading Assignment:

In preparation for Session No. 3, please read in *Public Speaking and Influencing Men in Business:*

Chapter II—"Self-Confidence Through Preparation"—Pages 31 through 62.

Please read also in *How to Win Friends and Influence People:*

"A Short-Cut to Distinction"—Pages 1 through 13.

"How This Book Was Written—and Why"—Pages 15 through 22.

Please be sure to read in *How to Stop Worrying and Start Living,* pages 29 through 45. Your talk at Session No. 12 should be based on your experiences in the next nine weeks in the application of the rules set forth in this book. Reading assignments in this book will be given you each week up to and including the thirteenth session.

Don't forget the "Speech Building" sections in *Public Speaking and Influencing Men in Business.*

Personality Improvement,
   Impromptu Speeches and
   Pantomimes ....6:00 to 8:00 p.m.

How to Win Friends...............8:00 to 10:40 p.m.

Date.............. ....

Instructor.......... ....

Personality Improvement, Impromptu Speeches and Pantomimes—6:00 to 8:00 p.m.

Personality is frequently the biggest single factor in business success. What is personality? It is the impression you make on other people. Clothes are a big factor in making that impression. True, clothes don't make the man, but they do make about ninety percent of all we see of the man. So tonight, a clothes counsellor will come to your class and tell you how to improve your personal appearance.

The clothes critic will be given seven minutes at the opening of the session for a talk about clothes. (NOTE, DIRECTORS: We mean *no more than seven minutes.* Please ring the bell on the clothes critic if he tries to talk longer than the allotted time.) He will talk, for example, about right and wrong color combinations, about what color tie and shirt to wear with blue suits, brown suits and gray suits.

After his talk, the clothes counsellor will tell you *privately* how you can improve your personal appearance. (For the sake of privacy, he will talk to you individually in a low voice at the back of the room or out in the hall or in an adjoining room.) He will discuss such personal problems as these: whether your

48

suit fits perfectly—especially whether it fits around the neck; whether your coat buttons need setting over a bit; whether you carry too many objects in your coat pockets; whether you ought to carry a pocket comb so that you can give your hair a bit of attention several times a day; whether you ought to carry a nail cleaner to keep your fingernails immaculate; whether your trousers are too long or too short; whether it is desirable to have pencils and fountain pens peeping out of your outside coat pocket; whether shirts with collars attached ought to have the collars starched a bit; whether you wear the kind of collar that is becoming to you; whether you wear the kind of suit that is becoming to you; whether your tie harmonizes with your shirt and suit; whether you ought to shine your shoes more often and have your suit pressed more frequently.

If the clothes counsellor is not able, during the 6:00 to 8:00 p.m. session, to give personal advice to every man who desires it, he will continue his personal interviews during the 8:00 to 10:40 p.m. session, until he has given every man an opportunity to find out how he can improve his dress and appearance.

Then Everyone Will Speak Impromptu

As soon as the clothes counsellor has finished his talk, each student will speak impromptu for 60 seconds.

Subjects?

The director will ask each student to write two suitable subjects on separate slips of paper. He will sort out the best ones and give them to class members. He will allow two minutes for students to think over the subjects—then will begin calling speakers.

Be sure to write good, easy subjects—because you may draw your own!

Don't try to make any formal speech on the subject given you. Instead, just say whatever jumps into your head, and out of your mouth. Don't try too hard on this one—just take it easy and have fun doing it—no catastrophies will happen if your talk isn't as good as Lincoln's Gettysburg speech.

Next a Pantomime Contest

The next event on the program tonight will be a pantomime contest. You should be prepared to tell a story (or describe an incident or an activity or a happening) with action only—no words whatever—that is, you tell your story by dumb show with significant gestures and facial expressions. Your pantomime *must* last at least 15 seconds—must not run over 45 seconds.

Tell a simple story. Here is an illustration—but it is best for you to work out a story of your own:

You come home from the office, reach in your pocket for the key to the door of your house or apartment. You can't find the key. You ring the door-bell. While your wife is coming to answer it, you still keep looking for your keys. She opens the door. You kiss her. Look toward the dining room. Sniff. Take the evening paper out of your pocket and start to read. Suddenly you read something that makes you mad. You throw the paper angrily across the room, go over to the chair in front of the radio, toss the cat out of the chair, sit down and tune in on program after program. All of them disgust you. Suddenly you tune in on an orchestra playing the Blue Danube. You jump up and waltz your wife around the room.

Remember that your story must be told with actions only—no words.

50

How the "Pantomime Champion" Is Selected

Your director will bring you up in groups of six to eight for the contest. After each member of a group has performed, the class will vote, by a show of hands, for the best pantomimist in that group. After all members of the class have performed, the group winners will be brought up and the class will vote again, by a show of hands, to decide who is the Pantomime Champion of the class.

What will you gain from this pantomime contest? It will get you out of your shell. It will loosen you up. It will train you to speak with your body as well as with words. It will tend to give you additional confidence, freedom and ease before an audience.

How to Win Friends—8:00 to 10:40 p.m.

Before the class members make their regular talks tonight, they will be put through, one by one, the "increasing feeling" warm-up. Each student will count 1, 2, 3, 4, and on up to perhaps 15 or 20. He should gradually increase the feeling he puts behind his words until he reaches the limit of his ability to say the words with more spirit and animation.

Perhaps you ask, as lots of students have, "What do you mean *feeling?*" Webster's answer is: "Any emotional state . . . as a *kindly* feeling." He defines *emotion* as: "Any one of the states designated as fear, anger, disgust, joy, surprise, yearning," etc.

So you will select some feeling or emotion and portray it as you count from one to perhaps 20. Maybe you will pick one of the emotions listed above. More probably, you will show some originality.

Some of the emotions portrayed the first time this stunt was tried were: anger—by a wife whose husband announces that he is stepping out to a stag party, leaving her at home to take care of the baby; distress —as the opposition makes the winning touchdown at a football game; anger—your date is late; mounting excitement—at a prize fight—a knockout; annoyance —when you are baby-sitting with a particularly pestiferous child; stage fright—as the time approaches to make an important speech; passing a graveyard at night—the gamut of confidence, fear, returning confidence.

Pick your own emotion and then increase it as you count. Just before you speak, please announce what emotion you are going to portray; and, if you wish, announce also the situation which is supposed to give rise to this emotion. You might say, for example, "Fear—I'm imagining that my foot is caught in the track and a train is approaching" or "Pride— student unexpectedly receiving the green pencil" or, for a laugh, "Love!"

To get the most out of this stunt:

1. Start speaking gently, quietly, in a hushed voice—let the first few numbers just roll out of your mouth.

2. As you increase the feeling you put into your speaking, try not to shout. Strive for *emotion,* rather than *noise.*

3. Gesture—otherwise you cannot possibly reach the peak of emotion.

This stunt will not only warm up the speakers, but will give them training in speaking with more power.

Your Human Relations Talk

You have by now read the introduction and parts one and two of Dale Carnegie's book, *How to Win*

Friends and Influence People—that is, the "Three Fundamental Techniques in Handling People" and the "Six Ways to Make People Like You."

We hope that you have been applying these principles. If you have done so, please tell us at this session how you applied them and what results you achieved.

We want you to do this for two reasons:

First, knowledge that is applied is the only kind that amounts to anything. If you don't use it, you will forget it. "The great aim of education," said Herbert Spencer, "is not knowledge, but action."

Why This Talk Will "Make Itself"

Second, if you applied the rules for winning friends, you obtained gratifying results, and you will come to the class with something that you *know* because you have *lived through it,* and with something that you really *want to tell.* Consequently, you will discover a great secret: You will find that, in these circumstances, you don't have to try to make a talk. You stand up and open your mouth and your message flows out of you like water rushing out of a fountain.

When you get into such a mental and emotional condition that you are *eager* to impart your message to your audience, you won't be frightened. You will forget yourself and you will make your hearers forget themselves. They will be conscious only of what you are saying. Under such circumstances, you are almost sure to make an excellent speech, and you will be surprised and delighted with your newly acquired ease, poise and personal effectiveness.

Most of these talks will be "examples"—that is, instances of how the human relations rules worked. You will hear a lot about "examples," beginning with the sixth session.

Of course, you don't *have* to talk about how you have applied the rules for winning friends. Our long experience tells us, however, that most of the good speeches made tonight will be based on the application of these "human relations" rules.

You will be allowed 90 seconds for this talk.

Three Books Awarded Tonight

Prizes will be presented tonight to the three people who make the best talks—three autographed copies of the book, *Lincoln the Unknown,* by Dale Carnegie. Even though you have won green, red or black pencils at previous sessions, you will be eligible to compete for these books. No other prizes will be given tonight.

The books will be awarded by secret ballot to the three students who have made the best talks on how they applied the rules for winning friends. Talks on other subjects will not be considered in the voting.

Please vote for the *three* you felt made the best talks and so deserve to be awarded the books. (Don't vote for one—vote for *three.*)

Dale Carnegie requests that the winner of each prize write out his speech, as best he remembers it, and mail it to him at 27 Wendover Road, Forest Hills, N. Y.

Have You a Topic for the "Coming Out of Your Shell" Session?

You should start right now to select a topic for the "Coming Out of Your Shell" session next week. See page 61 for suggestions. If you do not like any of these subjects, ask your class director for a suggestion. Take a subject you are enthusiastically for or against—think about it all week—get both sides of it—talk to your friends about it—then come to class prepared to deliver this talk with all of the feeling and intensity you possess. Let yourself go—dare to be yourself and express yourself and your views. If you will do this, you will gain enormously in self-confidence, ease and effectiveness.

Talks, Prizes and Reading Assignment
Session Number Four

Talks:

6:00 to 8:00 p.m. session — 60 seconds — Impromptu speech.

8:00 to 10:40 p.m. session—90 seconds—Talk on how you used one of the three "Fundamental Techniques in Handling People" or one of the "Six Ways to Make People Like You."

Prizes:

8:00 to 10:40 p.m. session—Copies of the book, *Lincoln the Unknown,* for the three best talks.

Reading Assignment:

In preparation for Session No. 4, please read in *Public Speaking and Influencing Men in Business:* Chapter III—"How Famous Speakers Prepared Their Addresses"—Pages 65 through 96.

Please be sure to review in *How to Win Friends and Influence People:*

Part I—"Fundamental Techniques in Handling People"—Pages 25 through 71.

Part II—"Six Ways to Make People Like You"—Pages 75 through 133.

Please read in *How to Stop Worrying and Start Living,* pages 46 through 66.

Please read the "Speech Building" sections at the end of the chapter assigned in *Public Speaking and Influencing Men in Business.*

┌───┐
│ **SESSION NO. 5** │
│ Capturing Your Audience ...6:00 to 8:00 p.m. │
│ Coming Out of Your Shell 8:00 to 10:40 p.m. │
│ Date .. │
│ Instructor .. │
└───┘

Capturing Your Audience—
6:00 to 8:00 p.m.

Tonight every member of the class will first give a 60-second talk on any subject he chooses. Our advice is: Give the same talk which you plan to give in the "Coming Out of Your Shell" session later in the evening. The better you know this talk, the easier it will be to bowl over the hecklers. So give yourself a dress rehearsal of that talk. Give it with all the animation and force and punch that you expect to use later. However, if you do not want to use the same speech twice, talk on whatever you like.

Now for the Two-Speaking-at-Once Contest

Next you will take part in a two-speaking-at-once contest—which you will find one of the most thrilling, amusing and helpful stunts of the entire course. The purpose of this contest is to help you to forget yourself and to think only of your audience and your message. It will help you to develop force and spontaneity in your speaking and it will get you loosened up and ready for the other speeches you will make tonight.

This stunt is a rapid-fire contest in which two speakers speak at the same time. Each one tries to win and hold, for 30 seconds, the attention of the audience.

56

Speak on any topic you like. Don't bother to get a new speech—use one of your old ones. This is no drill in speech construction, but an effort to get you to use animated and forceful delivery.

Here is how the contest is conducted: When the director shouts, "Go," you and another student will both face the same audience—and compete for the attention of that audience.

Start to speak instantly with zip and enthusiasm. Use gestures constantly. Vigorous gestures! Pay no attention to what the other speaker is saying or doing. Concentrate on your own job. Say to yourself, "I am going to make the audience listen to me instead of to him." Don't talk just to the people in front of you; talk to the back row, too, and to the people in front of the other speaker. Let all of them have both barrels.

The Director Is Referee and Judge

The director will stand near the two contestants, watch in hand. At the end of 30 seconds—or sooner, if either contestant weakens, he will shout, "Time." The director will determine the winner; or, if the contest is close, he will let the class decide by a show of hands. Please vote, not for the speaker who yelled loudest, but for the one who spoke with the most force and conviction. The loser will resume his regular seat. The winner will stay on the platform.

Then another pair speaks—then another—and so through the entire class. If the matching does not come out even, three people will speak at the end of the round. After all have spoken in the first round, the winners will be matched in the second round. Then the winners in the second round will be matched in the third—and so on to the finals, where the class champion is determined.

This stunt will be run off at high speed. To keep it going fast, your director will, before the contest starts, bring up all members of the class and have them stand at one side of the platform. He will have three assistants: (1) a "bringer-up" whose job it is to have two speakers standing right behind the contestants, who can start talking immediately after the winner of the previous contest is decided; (2) a man to pilot the winners across to the other side of the platform, where they will await their turn in the second round; (3) a man to steer the losers back to their seats in the audience. Why are these two "pilots" necessary? Because most people work up to such a pitch of excitement in this contest that they are likely to try to walk right through the side of the building!

You can safely look forward to this contest as one of the top spots of the entire course.

Coming Out of Your Shell—
8:00 to 10:40 p.m.

Tonight you will be drilled in saying the following sentences, which are often referred to humorously as the Dale Carnegie "college yell":

"I know men in the ranks who are going to stay in the ranks. Why? I'll tell you why—simply because they haven't the ability to get things done."

You will be required to say these sentences with the proper gestures and with gusto and enthusiasm. You will be drilled to pause in the right places and to change your pitch and your rate of speaking, so as to emphasize the important ideas. Your instructor will personally demonstrate how to say these sentences correctly; and then he will drill you in groups of six or eight to deliver them with force, with gestures,

58

with pauses, with sharp changes of pitch and abrupt changes of tempo. Please memorize these sentences now.

NOTE: *We do not believe in formal gestures. We require them in this warm-up only because we want to encourage students to use physical animation.*

Now for "Coming Out of Your Shell"

Hooray! Throw your hat in the air! You are going to have a lot of fun. Don't let this session disturb you. While you talk, people will perhaps interrupt you by asking questions—but you will be so excited over your talk, you will hardly hear them.

Why do we let listeners interrupt you? Is it because we want to train you to speak before hecklers? No! No! The chances are not one in ten thousand that you will ever have to speak before hostile hecklers. The real purpose of this session is to help you solve the biggest problem you face in this training: the problem of getting out of your shell and letting yourself go and talking naturally. Your problem is not to learn to talk. You could express your feelings superbly even when you were a child. You can express your ideas superbly now when you are in a hot argument. But when you face an audience, you draw into your shell like a turtle, you repress yourself. You become self-conscious and talk like a wooden Indian with an inferiority complex. You are afraid to gesture. You are afraid to use emphasis and feeling. You are afraid people will laugh at you.

Watch This Stunt Perform Miracles

Well, get this straight: *Tonight you must talk with wild enthusiasm—or else!!!*

To help you talk with enough animation, you will be asked to emphasize your remarks by banging on the table with a newspaper. Therefore, each student is requested to bring two newspapers to this session—to be used for "table-whacking."

If you will roll your newspaper up into a hard roll and fasten it at the ends with Scotch tape, tire tape or string, you will have a more efficient shillelagh. As you talk, you will gesture with all your might. To emphasize important words, phrases and sentences, you will whack the top of the table with your paper, whang it and beat it and lambaste it as if you were trying to smash it to atoms. (All rolled newspapers should be piled within your reach as you speak because you may wear out two or three and hence need replacements!)

As soon as you start speaking, your instructor, who will stand in the front of the room, will signal the students who have been assigned as "hecklers" to start asking you questions or making disparging remarks. However, just as soon as the instructor feels that you are really letting yourself go, he will call off the hecklers and will keep them silent—as long as you keep going a hundred miles an hour. If you slow up— if you weaken—he will call the gang back in again.

So it is really your choice. If you don't want to be disturbed with questions, just start in with wild enthusiasm—shout, wave your arms, talk right over the top of the hecklers—and the noise will be stopped. On the other hand, if you talk without feeling and enthusiasm and animation, you will be forced to face a barrage of questions and uncomplimentary remarks all the way through your talk.

We have asked instructors never to let more than three or four students pester you at any one time because the purpose of the session is defeated if the heckling becomes too loud.

Obviously, this is to be all in good fun; so please, when you are assigned to heckle, don't make any personal remarks that might wound the speaker's feelings. Underneath all the horseplay, let's use common sense.

What will you get out of this session? It will probably do more than any other one session to rid you of fear of people and audiences. It will blast you out of your reserve and give you a new sense of freedom and ease and command. Instead of fearing your listeners tonight, you will shake your fist at them and spurn them with contempt.

Be Sure to Have a Fighting Subject

If you want to get the most benefit out of this session, *be prepared.* Talk about something that makes you fighting mad. Give plenty of examples and details. Be specific. Illustrate your points. Talk about the time you bought a second-hand car that turned out to be a piece of junk; or about a raw deal that you got from some of your relatives; or about what happened when you lent money to your friends; or about a boss whom you hated; or a job that you despised; or a man who cheated you; or someone who insulted you.

Perhaps you are one of the unusual people who think you do not hate anybody or anything. Of course, that isn't quite true. You hate injustice, you hate intolerance, you hate the enemies of liberty, you hate cruelty to children and dumb animals. Surely the gentlest creatures on earth can find something they hate that they can talk about in this session.

As you talk, pound the desk. Tear your hair. Snort.

61

Breathe fire and brimstone. Raise your blood pressure forty points.

The speaker who comes nearest to having fits in front of the audience will get the prize for the best speech tonight.

Each student will speak for 60 seconds in the heckling session. Your instructor has been asked not to make any comments on speeches tonight. His main job is to encourage you to let yourself go.

As a closing event of a big evening, your instructor will ask you to repeat the talk you gave while you were being heckled—this time without the stimulation of questions or table-whacking. Try to put the same force, animation and enthusiasm into your talk that you did when you gave it earlier in the evening. Your instructor will try hard to get you to let yourself go, just as you did when you were wielding that roll of newspaper.

(Some instructors prefer to have each student make his "no-heckling" talk immediately after he has finished his "heckling" talk. This may be done in your class.)

How to Prepare for the Session Next Week

Tonight you will be given a booklet by Dale Carnegie entitled "How to Put Magic in the Magic Formula." This booklet explains and illustrates how to use this formula in a way that will help you get blowtorch results in public speaking, business conferences, sales letters, interviews, advertisements and talks at home with your wife and children.

We call this speech formula the "Magic Formula" because so many of our graduates have testified that it helped them get magic results when appealing for action.

This booklet will show you how to prepare your magic formula talk for next week. Please read this booklet tomorrow and start using the magic formula at once.

If you are absent from tonight's session, please call at the office and get a copy of the magic formula booklet.

Start Getting Ready for the Enthusiasm Session Now

Tonight you will also be given a booklet entitled "How One Idea Multiplied My Income and Happiness," by Frank Bettger, one of America's outstanding speakers on salesmanship. Regardless of whether you are a salesman, a housewife or an engineer, you can profit by reading this booklet. You need to read it as preparation for your talk at the ninth session.

You will be asked to tell the class in your speech in the 8:00 to 10:40 p.m. part of the ninth session what results you secured by acting with extraordinary enthusiasm.

In order to have something to talk about, we ask that you begin right now to act fully ten times as enthusiastically as you usually do and keep on doing it until you finish your talk in the enthusiasm session.

Please remember these two points: (1) the best way to become enthusiastic is to *act enthusiastic* and (2) the man who is enthusiastic can perform miracles.

So this practice of being enthusiastic day after day may work a real revolution in your life.

Start in right now turning on the enthusiasm. Anybody can do it who will keep thinking about it. Paste a note on your mirror: "Be more enthusiastic," so you can't help seeing it when you shave. Put a similar note on your desk at the office or your machine at the shop.

Tell your wife what you are doing and ask her to remind you—ditto for your assistant, your secretary, the gang at the plant.

Really *work* at this—because it may mean a lot to you.

Maybe some students will say, "I'm enthusiastic enough now—people couldn't stand me if I were any more enthusiastic." If you think you are enthusiastic enough, ask your directors for their opinions—and act on their judgment. Ten to one, they will tell you, "Be more enthusiastic."

If you really work at displaying lots of enthusiasm, you will surely have a wonderful story to tell when you face your class in the enthusiasm session.

Here's Where We Begin to Play Politics

Your class will hold a burlesque election in the second part of the eighth session. (For details, read the description of the session entitled "Campaign Talks" on pages 86-88 of this book.) Tonight, following the 8:00 to 10:40 p.m. session, your class director will divide the class into three parties, City Slickers, Country Hicks, and Cowboys, and will appoint a chairman for each party.

These three groups will then retire into different corners of the room and nominate three candidates. (In the United States, nominate candidates for governor, lieutenant-governor and state treasurer; in Canada, nominate city officials.) At the end of Session No. 6, the chairmen will appoint rousing speakers to make nominating addresses for their candidates at the election. Others will be appointed to make keynote speeches, seconding speeches and campaign speeches. In addition, each man nominated should be prepared

64

to accept the nomination with a speech. *Each speaker will be held strictly to two minutes.* Keep this rule in mind when you prepare your speech.

Talks, Prizes and Reading Assignment
Session Number Five　　•

Talks:

6:00 to 8:00 p.m. session—60-second talk—preferably the one you will give later in the "Coming Out of Your Shell" session; and also a 30-second talk to use in the two-speaking-at-once contest—on any subject about which you can speak forcefully.

8:00 to 10:40 p.m. session—60 seconds—Talk on some subject that makes you fighting mad.

Prizes:

8:00 to 10:40 p.m. session—Best speech, most improvement and special award pencils.

Reading Assignment:

In preparation for Session No. 5, please read in *Public Speaking and Influencing Men in Business:*

Chapter IV—"The Improvement of Memory"—Pages 99 through 131.

Chapter XIV—"How to Interest Your Audience"—Pages 419 through 448.

Please read in *How to Stop Worrying and Start Living,* pages 67 through 88.

SESSION No. 6
Eliminating "Word Whiskers" 6:00 to 8:00 p.m.
The Magic Formula...............8:00 to 10:40 p.m.
Date..
Instructor..

Eliminating "Word Whiskers"— 6:00 to 8:00 p.m.

You get two chances to talk tonight in the 6:00 to 8:00 p.m. session. First you make a 60-second talk on any subject you select. Then you will participate in a contest to help you eliminate "word whiskers."

HOW TO STOP USING "ERS"

by DALE CARNEGIE

What are "word whiskers"? They are the irritating "ers" and "uhs" and "mmms" that you have heard a thousand times not only in speeches, but also in conversation. Haven't you heard people talk in this manner: "Now let me see . . . uh . . . probably the wisest thing to do would be to . . . er . . . appoint a committee to . . . mmm . . . uh . . . to investigate this whole problem."

How can we eliminate "word whiskers"? First, we must find out the causes that produce them, and then eliminate the causes. The chief cause of "word whiskers" is that you start to speak before you know precisely what you want to say. When you do that, you may have to pause for thoughts. While you are pausing for thoughts, you are liable to break your silence with some "uhs" and "ers."

66

Think Only of What You Are Talking About

Another cause of "word whiskers" is that you try to talk when you are thinking of something other than what you are saying.

To eliminate "word whiskers," observe these two "don'ts":

1. Don't try to say one thing when you are thinking of something else.

2. Don't start to speak until you know what you want to say.

"Word Whisker" Contest

For the "word whisker" contest your class will be divided by the director into two groups, the "Ers" and the "Uhs." These groups will stand and face each other.

The class director in charge of the contest will give the first contestant a subject on which he must talk for 30 seconds. Thereafter, as soon as a contestant has finished speaking, he must at once call out a subject to the next speaker on the opposing side. Be sure to have your subject ready—unless you can produce it in five seconds, it will cost your side one point.

Any time you let fly with a "word whisker," the opposing team will snap their fingers. Each "word whisker" will count as a point against you and your team. The side with the lower score wins the contest.

You must give your subject verbally to your opponent—and remember, you are "on the air" until you have done this. If you "er" while you are giving the subject, it counts against you. Naturally, the more difficulty the student has in speaking on the subject assigned to him, the more he has to think about it as

67

he talks, and the more likely he is to "er"—and thus score a point against his team. So give your opponent some subject like "The Tariff," "How to Prevent War," "Love," "Hot Dogs," "Finger Nails"—and watch the fun. Don't give subjects which are either too easy or too difficult—the class director will be the judge and may require you to give your opponent another subject.

A class director will keep score—and announce which side won.

At future sessions, every time anyone is guilty of an "er" or an "uh," the members of the class should tap on their goblets or snap their fingers. As soon as students begin to hear their own "word whiskers," which will be within a few weeks under this treatment, they will tend to stop using them.

Here Are the Rules of the Contest

This "word whisker" contest is governed by these rules:

1. A "word whisker" does not count against a contestant unless his opponents snap their fingers to indicate that they caught the "er."

2. A student must start speaking within three seconds after he is given his subject. Penalty, one point.

3. He must continue speaking for the full 30 seconds. Penalty, one point.

4. If he pauses at any point in his talk for more than three seconds, a point will be scored against his team.

5. Each contestant must be ready to give a subject to an opponent immediately after his talk ends. Unless he can do so in five seconds, this failure will cost his team one point.

6. One of the class directors will act as referee. He will decide all doubtful cases, as for example, whether you perpetrated a "grunt" or an "er"! He will also have the right to reject any subject if it is, in his judgment, either too difficult or too easy and require the contestant to give his opponent a satisfactory subject.

You Can Render Us a Great Service

Do you know any friends or acquaintances who would benefit by taking the Dale Carnegie Course? If so, would you be willing to give us their names?

The only names that will be of real service to us are those of people with whom you have talked about the course—people who have shown some interest.

Your director will hand you tonight sheets on which you can write the names and addresses of your friends who might like to take the course. Your name will not be used unless you give us written permission. We will invite these people to the next open meeting so that they can learn for themselves whether or not the Dale Carnegie Course is what they want and need.

Please fill out this form tonight and hand it to your director or take it home and bring it back to class next week.

The Magic Formula—8:00 to 10:40 p.m.

Last week you were given a booklet by Dale Carnegie entitled "How to Put Magic in the Magic Formula." (If you were absent and did not receive this booklet by mail, please call at or telephone the headquarters of the Dale Carnegie Course in your city and secure your copy.)

This magic formula is something you will use the

rest of your life. You will use it every time you try to persuade someone to do something—because:

1. It is a formula for straight and logical thinking.

2. It is the natural and normal way of presenting your case.

Tonight you are to deliver three steps (point, reason and example) of a speech in which you ask your audience *to do something*. This speech may be about any subject you wish, but it must be based on the magic formula and hence must *ask for action by the audience*. If your point *does not* request action, your instructor will say, "What do you want us to do?" and will keep on saying it until he gets from you a point that does ask for action. For further details, see *How to Put Magic in the Magic Formula*.

This formula, part of which you will use tonight, is a magic formula not only for talks; it is also a magic formula for writing letters, advertisements and circulars.

As you will learn by reading *How to Put Magic in the Magic Formula*, the complete formula consists of five steps: *ho hum*, point, reason, example, *so what*.

Prepare Only Part of Your Talk for Tonight

Tonight we want you to prepare only three of the five steps of the formula—the "middle three"—point, reason and example. Next week you will put a *ho hum* in front of the point-reason-example speech which you prepared for this week and a *so what* at the end, and you will have a complete magic formula talk (*ho hum*, point, reason, example, *so what*).

Remember, though—tonight you prepare only your point, reason and example. You will be allowed one and a half minutes to deliver this talk.

70

Before you speak tonight, your instructor will help the class develop some point-reason-example speeches that are suitable for magic formula talks. This is just to demonstrate how easy it is to use the magic formula.

We Go to Work on Your Speech

Then your instructor will check the point, reason and example of every member of the class—to see if the three steps follow the rules. He will start with the first person in the front row (or maybe the last person in the last row, or right in the middle—so don't try to outguess him and sit where you will not be called on until last!) and ask that person to give his point and reason and a few words of his example.

When your turn comes, you should give your three steps in skeleton form—just enough so that the instructor can decide whether or not your first two steps are satisfactory and your third (example) is relevant and suitable. You will say: "My point is . . .; my reason is . . .; my example, in brief, is . . ."

If the three items are O.K., the instructor will say so. If not, he will go to work on your speech and will continue working, with help from the class, until he has helped you to develop a satisfactory point, reason and example. Then he will pass on to the next student and so on until he has completed the round of the class.

Be Sure to Make the Suggested Improvements

It will take until recess time to do this job. If, when the instructor checked your point, reason and example, he or any class member made suggestions that would improve your talk, you should use the recess time to revise your speech to include the suggested improvements. For instance, if the instructor points out that your example is not relevant and helps you to get a new one that is relevant, be sure to use the new, not the old, example in your after-recess talk. If you do not understand the suggestions or need any help, ask the instructor or one of the directors to help you in the recess period.

After recess you will have 90 seconds to deliver the three steps of your talk—point, reason and example—in full.

Please note that your point should be a request for action—since this is an action speech. Don't use as a point: "The Red Cross is a great humanitarian organization"—say, instead, "Give to the Red Cross." Don't say, "Health and accident insurance is worth what it costs"—say, instead, "Take out health and accident insurance." That is, ask the audience to do something.

You would not necessarily follow this rule if you were making a speech in public. You might take as your point: "Socialized medicine is a noble institution" and for your reason, "because it makes it possible for the poor man to get just as good medical attention as the rich man." But in these class sessions, your instructor can be of the greatest help to you if you ask for action in your point. (Of course, you do not have to be as specific and go into as much detail in the point as you do in the *so what*.)

Once you have a point which asks for action, it is easy enough to think of a satisfactory reason. Then you have to secure an example.

The Example Is Most Important

The general purposes of an example are to make your talk:

(a) interesting   (c) clear

(b) convincing   (d) memorable

72

Specifically, the purpose of an example is to support (or back up) your point and reason. Actually, it is *testimony* (oral evidence) which tends to prove your point and reason. The kind of examples most commonly used in students' speeches is the *incident* or *episode* type—the type in which the speaker describes something that has happened. Of course, the relating of an incident is not the only testimony you can give to support your point and reason. You may use facts, statistics, expert testimony, demonstrations, exhibits or analogies.

Some Suggestions About Your Example

Here are a few suggestions about your example which will help you:

1. It must be short enough to fit into a two-minute speech, but long enough to be interesting. (A one or two-sentence example rarely has enough background and enough specific facts to be interesting.)

2. If you use the incident type of example, it should be a real incident—not an imaginary one. (An example you made up or one that begins with "suppose" or "if" is rarely convincing.)

3. It must be specific—must give facts. (Don't start this way: "Once a friend of mine and I went fishing." That is not specific enough. Who is your friend? When did you go? Where did you go? This example would be improved if you said, "Last Labor Day a friend of mine, John J. Jones of Smithville, went out to Lake Smith, just north of Smithville, to do some fishing.")

4. It must be relevant—it must be evidence that exactly supports your point and reason—it must be pertinent and applicable to that particular reason.

73

In selecting an example, always ask yourself, "Just exactly what am I trying to prove?" Suppose you were speaking on the point: "If you are going to college, you ought to learn how to speak in public"; and suppose your reason is: "As a result of learning to speak in public, you can make more effective oral recitations and thus get better marks." Then you would ask yourself, "Do I know anyone who, as a result of learning to speak in public, made better oral recitations and hence got better marks in college?" If you do, you can undoubtedly use that person's experience as an instance.

Please do not settle back and say, "My example is all right." No, before you come to class tonight, please check up on it. Do it by stating your point and reason —then asking yourself, "Does that example exactly back up my reason?" If it does, use it; if it doesn't, change it for one that does.

Try to use an incident that has life and action and motion. Preferably get one out of your own experience or the experience of someone you know well.

Pick a Simple Subject

A word of warning—in preparing your speech for tonight, don't ask your audience to do something big —to save democracy, to prevent future wars or to balance the budget. Why? Because to deal intelligently with these complex subjects, you need, not the 90 seconds that you have in this class, but one hour—yes, maybe one day or one year. So ask your audience to do something simple, such as buying your product, being more patient with the children, or applying some of the principles discussed in *How to Win Friends and Influence People*. Appeal for action about some simple thing that you know about from your

74

own experience. Make it easy. Make it short. Remember, you will have only 90 seconds in which to deliver your point, reason and example.

Get Ready for the Election Session

Tonight the chairmen of the campaign committees will appoint the speakers for the election in Session No. 8.

Have You Started Acting Enthusiastic?

If you get nothing else out of this course except the ability to feel and display real enthusiasm, you will get your money's worth — many times over! Please realize that you can never succeed completely unless you re-enforce your natural ability with real enthusiasm. You need it not only in your speaking, but in your conversation, your writing, your business, your profession, your social life and your home life.

Have you acted on the advice given you last week—the advice that you start at once acting ten times as enthusiastic as you normally do? Remember, you are doing this for two reasons:

1. By acting enthusiastic you tend to become enthusiastic.

2. If you act wildly enthusiastic, you will have a wonderful story to tell in Session No. 9 as to what enthusiasm has done for you—a story you can tell with real enthusiasm.

Please give this suggestion a fair trial—and please begin NOW—if you haven't begun already!

Talks, Prizes and Reading Assignment
Session Number Six

Talks:

6:00 to 8:00 p.m. session—Two talks in this ses-

75

sion: No. 1, 60 seconds—Any subject you select.
No. 2, 30 seconds—Subject assigned in "Word
Whisker" contest.

8:00 to 10:40 p.m. session—90 seconds—Prepare
point, reason and example, only, of a speech in
which you ask the audience to do something.

Prizes:

No prizes tonight.

Reading Assignment:

In preparation for Session No. 6, please read in
Public Speaking and Influencing Men in Business:

Chapter XV—"How to Get Action"—Pages 451
through 483.

Also, be sure to reread and study the booklet you
received last week—the booklet by Dale Carnegie
entitled "How to Put Magic in the Magic Formula."

Please read in *How to Stop Worrying and Start Living,* pages 89 through 120.

```
┌─────────────────────────────────────────────┐
│            SESSION No. 7                       │
│ Thinking Out Your Talk..........6:00 to  8:00 p.m.│
│ You Learn About Ho Hums and                    │
│    So Whats ........................8:00 to 10:40 p.m.│
│                                                │
│ Date........................................... │
│                                                │
│ Instructor....................................... │
└─────────────────────────────────────────────┘
```

Thinking Out Your Talk—6:00 to 8:00 p.m.

Before you make your regular talk tonight, you will be asked to rise, stand at your chair and say the ABC's with great gusto and enthusiasm. You will be drilled until you put feeling and emotion into your reciting of the alphabet. You will be drilled to use vigorous gestures and to say the alphabet as if it were, to you, the most vital thing in the world. After that exaggeration, your regular talk will seem easy.

Now for Your Speeches

What will you talk about tonight? Any subject on which you have *earned the right to talk*. You will have 90 seconds for this speech.

Reread the booklet, *A Quick and Easy Way to Learn to Speak in Public*. You will surely get some good subjects from it.

Maybe One of These Subjects Will Suit You

If you want us to suggest a subject, how about this one: "*What Is Right and What Is Wrong with Our Stores?*" Imagine that you have been invited to speak at a banquet of retail merchants. They are eager to improve their methods—especially their relations with

77

customers. They have asked you to tell them what is right and what is wrong with their clerks, their executives, their stores, their advertising, their goods. They tell you they will welcome any criticism—constructive or destructive. They invite you to tell all! So tell them! Be guided in doing so, however, by the nine rules for changing people without giving offense which will be found on page 164 of this book.

Please remember also to give an illustration of each point you make. If you are talking about discourteous clerks, be specific. Give an example of how you were badly treated by a clerk in some retail store.

If you don't want to talk about stores, why not tell us whether it is better to buy a new car or a used car. People have been debating this question, without decision, for over twenty-five years. If you have any opinion on the subject, here is your chance to make a strong talk.

Or maybe you can get all lathered up about the liquor question—for or against.

Here's another sure-fire subject: "Courtesy and Discourtesy I've Met at the Hands of Policemen."

Perhaps you have another subject which you like better; if so, use it.

Of Course You Have Something to Say

You may think that you have nothing to say on the subjects listed above—or any subject. Perhaps you haven't right now. But pick the one you like best and start preparing your speech as follows:

1. Think about it in your spare time.

2. Make notes of all ideas that occur to you.

3. Talk the subject over with your friends.

4. *Think* it out. (Are you afraid that, when you face the audience, you will forget what to say? If so, make a few notes and, if necessary, glance at them occasionally as you talk, but don't *write out* your talk.)

The most important of the rules we give above is "Think it out." If you do think it out, you will find that one thought will lead to another. Ideas will accumulate. Illustrations and examples will flash into your mind. In a few days, you will have enough material to last far more than ninety seconds.

Remember, speeches don't spring full grown from your forehead. They develop slowly and they grow day and night, like a child.

How to Test the Speeches Tonight

As each speaker talks tonight, will you please hold this Red Book in your hand and ask, about his talk, the seven questions listed below. If the answer is *NO* to most of the questions, the talk has probably been a failure.

Here are the questions:

As to the speaker—

1. Does he know thoroughly what he is talking about—has he earned the right to talk on that subject?
2. Is he genuinely interested in it himself?
3. Is he eager to get his message over to his audience?
4. Is he having a good time giving his talk?

As to the speech—

5. Does it have a point?
6. Is it clear?
7. Is the point illustrated by an example?

Of course, if you are speaking about some sad or unpleasant subject—obviously you won't be expected to have a good time making your talk. Such speeches are the exception.

Generally speaking, remember that, unless you have a good time giving your talk, your audience will not have a good time listening to it.

You can largely control the attitude of your audience toward what you say. How? By controlling your own attitude. If you are enthusiastic, your hearers will tend to be enthusiastic. If you are indifferent, your hearers will be indifferent. Your attitude is contagious.

You Learn About *Ho Hums* and *So Whats*— 8:00 to 10:40 p.m.

Tonight you will deliver a complete five-step magic formula talk. In preparation, please reread and study carefully the five *ho-hums* recommended in the booklet, *How to Put Magic in the Magic Formula*. In fact, you ought to reread this entire booklet several times before you start to prepare your talk for tonight.

Before your instructor hears your talks, he will check the *ho-hums* and *so whats* of class members, to be sure they are satisfactory. Every time he finds one that isn't, he will call on class members to help the student find one which is.

Since it is a long, slow process—but a very worthwhile one—to provide every speaker with a satisfactory *ho-hum*, it is likely to be recess time—and a late recess at that—before it is done.

After the instructor has been around the class and is sure that all persons there have *ho hums* that arouse the interest of the audience and *so whats* that ask for specific, easy, possible action, he will have each of you deliver your finished speech in two minutes. He will have no time to comment on anything except how you used the formula. "O.K." is the highest praise you can hope for tonight—and that's high praise indeed. The instructor will comment on your talk only if there is something wrong with it—in which case he will make you do over again—correctly—the part that did not conform to our rules.

For your talk tonight, take the three-step talk you used last week and put an opening (or *ho hum*) on the front of it and a request for action (or *so what*) on the end of it—then deliver the finished product in two minutes—with a lot of animation and, incidentally, a lot of pride — because it will be a rip-whooping action talk.

Tonight, please be sure you have all five steps in your talk and that you deliver them in the regular order: *ho hum,* point, reason, example and *so what.* As is explained in the booklet, *How to Put Magic in the Magic Formula,* you do not have to use all five steps in ordinary public speaking you do outside the class, or to have them in the conventional order. However, your instructor and your class members will be able tonight to give you the most help if you will present your talk with five steps, in the requested order.

However else you open your talk, please be sure you do not make the mistake that Dale Carnegie warns you against in *How to Put Magic in the Magic Formula*—the mistake of opening it with a dull, trite, preachy, stereotyped or too-obvious statement. After you have thought of an opener, ask yourself, "Has it been said a couple of million times?" If so, discard it. (You know what we mean: "Early to bed and early to rise," "Honesty is the best policy"—old truisms of that sort.) Ask yourself if it is too obvious—too evident. If so, it will never interest the audience. (For example: "If you murder someone, you will get into trouble," "Every man ought to be patriotic"—hair-raising statements like that.)

Dale Carnegie also warns you against the too sensational opener, and the "funny story" opener.

Rarely Open Your Talk With a Question

Please do not open your talk by asking a question unless you are certain that it will interest the audience. Please do not use a show-of-hands opener if the question you ask is dull or obvious. (Example: "How many people in this audience would like to have a million dollars? Let me see your hands." Of course, practically everybody would like a million dollars, so this opener is silly and ineffectual.)

Be sure that your *ho hum* fits the rest of the talk— is relevant. It is not enough merely that it interests the audience—it must lead naturally into the next step of your talk.

Also, please be sure that the *so what* you select is specific, is within the power of the audience to do and is easy to do.

Here's Some Important Advice

Please remember that, in preparation for the enthusiasm session, No. 9, you are going to act all day, every day, about ten times as enthusiastic as normal— and be ready to tell, at the ninth session, what you did and how people reacted to your more enthusiastic behavior.

82

Talks, Prizes and Reading Assignment
Session Number Seven

Talks:

6:00 to 8:00 p.m. session—90 seconds—Talk on some subject you will enjoy talking about and on which you have *earned the right to talk.*

8:00 to 10:40 p.m. session—2 minutes—Make a complete magic formula talk.

Prizes:

8:00 to 10:40 p.m. session—Best speech, most improvement and special award pencils.

Reading Assignment:

In preparation for Session No. 7, please read in *Public Speaking and Influencing Men in Business:*

Chapter IX—"How to Open a Talk"—Pages 261 through 291.

Chapter XI—"How to Close a Talk"—Pages 325 through 350.

Please read also in *How to Win Friends and Influence People:*

Part III—"Twelve Ways to Win People to Your Way of Thinking"—Pages 137 through 218.

Please read in *How to Stop Worrying and Start Living,* pages 121 through 148.

Don't forget "Speech Building" at the end of each chapter assigned in *Public Speaking and Influencing Men in Business.*

```
┌─────────────────────────────────────────────┐
│              SESSION No. 8                    │
│ Thinking on Your Feet............6:00 to 8:00 p.m. │
│ Campaign Talks .............8:00 to !!!!      │
│                                              │
│ Date.......................................... │
│                                              │
│ Instructor.................................... │
└─────────────────────────────────────────────┘
```

Note Change in Order of Sessions

In all sessions except this one, the part of the session handled by the directors comes first—from 6:00 to 8:00 p.m.; the part handled by the instructor comes later—from 8:00 to 10:40 p.m. For tonight only, this order is reversed: The instructor is in charge of the first part and the directors are in charge of the second part. This change is made to allow more time for the election session.

Thinking on Your Feet—
6:00 to 8:00 p.m.

The chief purpose of tonight's session is to enable you to discover for yourself how easy it is to keep going for 90 seconds without any formal preparation whatever—when you are speaking about something that you know, something that you want to talk about, something that you spent five or ten years earning the right to talk about.

When the class assembles tonight, you will be given a sheet which contains a list of subjects that you will find easy to discuss. Select any subject you wish, so long as you feel you have earned the right to talk about it. Tell what you know about the subject from your own experience and observation. If you do that, you will probably make a far better talk than you now imagine you can. If you don't like the subjects on the list handed to you by your instructor, ask him to give you another subject.

Should you follow the magic formula in this speech? Yes, if you are making a speech that asks for action —that asks the audience to do something. If you decide on such a talk, follow these steps:

As soon as you have selected your subject, ask yourself how you stand on that subject. You probably don't have to ask yourself how you stand on some subjects, such as divorce—you *know*. Suppose you favor more strict divorce laws and want to ask your fellow students to make speeches against too-liberal divorce laws—then that is your point. Naturally you must support that with a reason. Then you start to think of an example to support your point and reason. Then you ask for action in the closing sentence of your talk—your *so what*. If you have time, you will then work out a *ho hum*. If you haven't time, you will start with your point.

Your big problem will be to get a satisfactory example, so here's a suggestion: Try to pick a point and reason for which you can easily supply an example.

If you do not make a speech in which you ask for action, use such parts of the magic formula as are applicable.

Read—And Reread This Booklet

As preparation for your talk tonight, be sure to reread and study the booklet, *A Quick and Easy Way to Learn to Speak in Public.* You were given a copy of this booklet at the second session of the course; and you ought to read it once a week in every week of this course.

If You Forget This, You'll Be Sorry!

You will talk at the ninth session on your experiences with super-enthusiasm. To have experiences, you will have to use the rule: "Be ten times as enthusiastic as normal."

If you haven't gone to work on this rule, please start now. If you have, just keep it up. It pays enormous dividends on a small investment.

Campaign Talks—8:00 to !!!

Every man or woman is likely to be called on at some time to speak in favor of a candidate for office. Tonight you will learn how to make campaign speeches—and probably will have more fun and excitement than you have had in years.

There'll be a hot time in the old town tonight. Big excitement! Big election! Three sets of candidates will plead for your vote tonight—the City Slickers, the Country Hicks and the Cowboys! Nominating speeches will be made! Seconding speeches! Speeches by the rival candidates telling how they propose, if elected, to save the nation, to lower taxes and to balance the budget. Don't talk over two minutes—because the bell will be working as usual. No firearms will be allowed at the session tonight, and the bar in the hotel should be closed!

WARNING—This is in no sense a heckling session. Every speaker should be allowed to make his speech without interruptions or comments from his audience. The class director in charge is asked to enforce the no-heckling rule.

What a Night This Is!

Come prepared to make rousing, vote-getting talks for your favorite candidates. What a session! Some-

times the parties parade—the City Slickers in paste-
board plug hats, the Cowboys in 5-gallon sombreros
and chaps, the Rubes in straw hats and overalls!
Banners! Placards! Handbills! Campaign songs!
Posters! One cigar manufacturer, who was taking the
course, supplied campaign cigars with the name of his
party on the bands. One class broadcast through the
hotel radio. Another hired a band! Parades—one led
by a "two-way" horse with one man in the front legs
and another in the hind legs. Handshaking—back-
slapping—electioneering!

Don't be surprised if, on the final vote, it proves
that no one is elected. Perhaps the ballot box was
stuffed or stolen. Remember this is a burlesque!

How men and women do love an election—and
how they revel in this one! Bring your friends—so
they can enjoy the fun.

Remember, don't make this session too elaborate.
The session can't possibly last for more than three or
four hours. Don't go to too much trouble and expense.
Remember, it's all in fun.

Visitors Are Invited Tonight

Each member is invited to bring visitors tonight. In
this way, you will have a new and larger audience on
which to practice.

Don't, DON'T Memorize Your Talk

Some students make the serious mistake of writing
out and memorizing their election night speeches.
Don't, don't, don't do that. If you do, your talk is
bound to sound memorized and lifeless. Your memorized talk will not sound like one human being saying something he means to other human beings. In-

stead, it will sound like precisely what it is: memorized words. Memorized words rarely do anything to an audience except bore it.

Think out your election talk tonight. Go over it many times in your mind. When you start to speak, have a good time. Put life and good humor in it. Suppose you do forget something you intended to say—so what? No one will know it but yourself. Keep right on. Say something—anything and say it fast. Have a rip-roaring good time.

Talks, Prizes and Reading Assignment
Session Number Eight

Talks:

6:00 to 8:00 p.m. session—90 seconds—Impromptu talk.

8:00 to 10:40 p.m. session—2 minutes—Election session talks.

Prizes:

6:00 to 8:00 p.m. session—Best speech, most improvement and special award pencils.

Reading Assignment:

In preparation for Session No. 8, please read in *Public Speaking and Influencing Men in Business:*

Chapter V—"Keeping the Audience Awake"—Pages 135 through 163.

Don't forget the sections on "Speech Building" in the above mentioned textbook.

Please read in *How to Stop Worrying and Start Living,* pages 149 through 166.

```
┌──────────── SESSION No. 9 ────────────┐
│ This Stunt Is Fun—                       │
│   And Helpful, Too............6:00 to  8:00 p.m. │
│ How to Make the Magic of                 │
│   Enthusiasm Work for You...8:00 to 10:40 p.m. │
│                                          │
│ Date.................................................. │
│                                          │
│ Instructor............................................ │
└──────────────────────────────────────────┘
```

This Stunt Is Fun—And Helpful, Too—
6:00 to 8:00 p.m.

Until you get over your self-consciousness, you will never be at your best in conversations, in conferences and in speeches.

Tonight your director will put you through a stunt which will help you to learn how to talk without thinking about yourself.

This is the stunt: You are to make a talk in which you burlesque some movie actor, radio announcer, political speaker, instructor, director, class member or, perhaps best of all, yourself.

"What do you mean by *burlesque?*" some students ask. Webster defines "burlesque" as: "literary, dramatic or other imitation which makes a travesty" (or "grotesque parody" or "ridiculous imitation") "of that which it represents; ludicrous or broadly humorous caricature."

Your *burlesque* should be a ludicrous imitation of someone.

Of course you can do it!

Does some member of your class talk too rapidly? Then you can burlesque his delivery by delivering a

89

talk at top speed. Does some class member use too many "ers"? You can burlesque him by making a talk in which you put an "er" before every word. Does somebody you know start every speech with an apology? You can burlesque him by making a longer, more abject, more unnecessary and sillier apology. Does some student walk up and down the platform as he speaks? Burlesque him by making a talk as you run madly up and down the platform. Is some instructor too ponderous and school-teachery? Burlesque him by pretending to comment on a student's talk with three times as much ponderosity. Is one of the girls in your class a "gusher"? You can burlesque her by making a talk that is all gush. Do any one of these things and you have a burlesque.

Perhaps the most effective burlesque of all is one of yourself. What are your worst speaking faults? Do you speak too fast or too slowly, too loud or too low? Do you gesture too much or too little? Do you talk in a monotone? Do you get mixed up and say the wrong thing? Think up two or three of your worst faults. Then figure out how you can exaggerate them—and you have a burlesque.

Surely it is an easy matter to make a wonderful burlesque talk—and that's what we expect you to do tonight.

You will be required to make a burlesque talk that lasts at least 30 seconds—you may have up to 120 seconds.

After the first round of talks you will probably have time for a second round—perhaps, for a third. You will find that the second time you do it, it will be easier—and the third time, still easier.

How to Make the Magic of Enthusiasm Work for You—8:00 to 10:40 p.m.

TO SUCCEED, HAVE ENTHUSIASM!

by Dale Carnegie

I once interviewed Charles Sumner Woolworth. He and his brother, Frank Woolworth, founded the five-and-ten-cent store industry. We got to talking about the factors that make for success, and Mr. Woolworth said, "A man can't succeed at anything unless he has enthusiasm for it."

That is just as true of speaking as it is of merchandising. Yes, after listening to and criticizing over a hundred and twenty thousand talks, I have come to the conclusion that no man can succeed in speaking unless he has enthusiasm. As far as the delivery of a speech is concerned, the two most important qualities by far are sincerity and enthusiasm.

You hold in the palm of your hand the attitude of your hearers toward what you are saying; their attitude is bound to be a reflection of your attitude. If you are bored, they will be bored. If you are lackadaisical, they will be lackadaisical. But if you are excited about what you are saying, if you are on fire with enthusiasm, your listeners can't keep from catching some of your inspiration. Enthusiasm is as contagious as the measles—and twice as much fun. Speaking for myself, I know that any little measure of success that I may have had in training men to speak, has been due far more to enthusiasm than to superior intelligence. You can go to Harvard and Princeton and take forty courses in public speaking, but unless you put enthusiasm into your talking, you will be like a woodpecker pecking on a dead tree.

91

The Man with Enthusiasm Wins

A few years ago, Frederick Williamson, who was then president of the New York Central Railroad, declared that enthusiasm was "the little-recognized secret of success." Mr. Williamson, a Yale graduate, was an extraordinarily conservative man. He didn't entertain half-baked theories or go off half-cocked. Yet when I asked him, in a radio interview, what he thought was the secret of success, he replied, "The longer I live, the more certain I am that enthusiasm is the little-recognized secret of success. The difference in actual skill and ability and intelligence, between those who succeed and those who fail, is usually neither wide nor striking. But if two men are nearly equally matched, the man who is enthusiastic will find the scales tipped in his favor. And a man of second-rate ability with enthusiasm will often outstrip one of first-rate ability without enthusiasm."

Yes, and a speaker of second-rate mental ability with enthusiasm will often outstrip a speaker of first rate mental ability without enthusiasm. I know. I have seen it happen hundreds of times. I am not theorizing. I am reporting facts, facts that I have observed personally.

You're Not as Enthusiastic as You Think

Is it easy to get students to speak with enthusiasm? Easy? It has been the most trying problem I have ever faced as an instructor. Why? Because in some cases, students have nothing that they are interested in saying. In other cases, they make the mistake of trusting their own ears. They feel they are using sufficient animation when they are not.

92

Three Ways to Develop Enthusiasm in Your Speaking

Tonight's session will be devoted to helping you speak with enthusiasm.

Here are three stunts that you will be asked to do tonight that will help you to put enthusiasm— "the little-recognized secret of success"—into your speaking:

1. Shake Yourself Awake

As a preliminary warm-up tonight, stand facing the class and pound your chest like an old gorilla—or do a bit of shadow boxing. That is what Houdini did. Houdini always shadow boxed before he stepped out on the stage to give his matchless performance of magic. He shadow boxed to warm himself up.

You need to shake yourself out of your lethargy, to pound your chest and send the red blood racing through your arteries. You need to put life and lilt and eagerness into your mental and emotional processes. . . . When I say pound your chest, I really mean *pound*. But don't knock yourself out. I almost did that one night in Seattle, Washington, while demonstrating to my listeners how to shake themselves awake. I hit myself so hard that I injured a rib, had to go to a doctor and wear tape for days.

So for a few seconds before you start your talk tonight, please swing your arms around in wide circles over your head. (Your instructor will signal you to stop when he thinks you have had enough—which will be as soon as your color has been heightened a trifle, but before you are winded.) If you don't like to swing your arms, try any of these exercises: Jump up and down, skip an imaginary rope, pitch a few fast ones, touch your fingers to the floor without bending your knees, shadow box or take any other violent

93

exercise you prefer. Ridiculous? Yes. Under ordinary circumstances, even a congenital idiot would not act that way; and you are going to feel like an idiot yourself when you do it in class tonight. But never mind. It is what you need. It will warm you up.

If your physical condition makes it undesirable for you to take violent exercise, please tell the instructor, who will excuse you from this stunt.

2. Give Yourself a Pep Talk

H. V. Kaltenborn, the famed radio news analyst, told me that when he was a young man, he found himself stranded in Paris; so, for a year, he sold stereoscopes and stereopticon views from house to house; and he couldn't speak French. At first, he despised the job so he gave himself a pep talk every morning. He looked into the mirror and said to himself, "Kaltenborn, you have to do this if you want to eat. So you might as well enjoy it. Do it with gusto and enthusiasm. Imagine that you are acting a part on the stage, because what you are doing is just as funny as something on the stage." He talked himself into enjoying his work. As a result, he made five thousand dollars in commissions that year. He told me that, in addition, this selling experience proved to be as valuable to him as any one year he spent in Harvard.

Since Kaltenborn's pep talks did so much for him, we are going to ask you to give the idea a whirl.

As soon as the instructor feels that you are "warmed up" and ready to start like a rocket bomb, he will ask you to give yourself a pep talk ALOUD. Speak for at least 15 seconds—but not more than 30 seconds.

Can You Give Yourself a Pep Talk?

Do you know how to give yourself a pep talk? To our astonishment, we find that many people have

94

never given themselves a pep talk in their lives and don't know how.

Here's a sample pep talk: "Jimmy, old boy, you have certainly earned the right to talk on this subject. You have been thinking about it, living it, sleeping it, eating it for fifteen years. You sure have deep feelings on this subject. So stand up and pour it on this audience. Let yourself go. Give! Don't think of yourself at all. Just think of how you can help the people in this audience by convincing them of this point. All right, let's go."

We don't want you to follow this pattern too closely, but we do want you to give yourself a good talking to —the sort of speech a football coach gives his team between halves of a close game. This pep talk should help to key you up to such a pitch that you can make a strong, effective, enthusiastic speech.

While you are giving yourself this pep talk, please gesture violently—for gestures will help you to put feeling and enthusiasm into what you are saying.

3. Force Your Audience to Sit Down

The real test of whether you need more enthusiasm, is not what *you* think about it, but what *your listeners* think about it. So tonight we are going to have four or five members of the audience stand up when each speaker starts to talk—the instructor or director will indicate which students are to stand. These standing listeners will act as a sort of steam gauge for you. They will continue to stand until your steam pressure rises to about eighty pounds per square inch; then they will sit down. Your task tonight will be to force your group of standing listeners to sit down as quickly as possible and *stay* down. If your steam pressure drops as you chug along, your human steam gauges will pop

95

up again; and you will have to stoke your fires once more.

Unfortunately, what usually happens at this session is this: When one of the standing listeners sits down, all the others sit down automatically. Please don't do that. Please don't act like sheep. Pay no attention to whether the others are standing or sitting. Trust your own judgment. Be tough—keep on standing until the speaker talks with so much enthusiasm that you just have to sit down. On the other hand, be fair—sit down when the speaker talks with real enthusiasm.

Your Subject Is Your Own Experience

What are you going to talk about? You are going to tell us, in two minutes, your experiences in displaying more enthusiasm. You will remember that we asked you, in Session No. 5, to begin the experiment of displaying a lot of enthusiasm and to be ready to tell the class tonight how the experiment worked.

If you acted on our advice, what a story you have to tell—a story of miracles, because enthusiasm surely does work miracles!

So tell us how you displayed enthusiasm and the results you got. Make it specific. Don't say, "As a result of being more enthusiastic, I was more popular at home, I did better work, I was happier." Those are all generalities—and as dull as generalities generally are. Instead, say something like this: "Let me tell you how it worked out. The first day, I got up with a bounce, sang while I dressed, found I had ten minutes to play with the children before I left for the office. Then I went off whistling. Of course my wife called up in a few minutes to ask if I was all right—but I was," etc., etc.

96

If you really worked at being enthusiastic, you will have a story to tell that you can tell with boiling enthusiasm. If you didn't work at it, you may have had some experience in the past where enthusiasm produced miraculous results for you. If so, use this incident as your subject. Be sure to reach a high point of enthusiasm in relating your story.

Perhaps you are one who will say, "I haven't acted very enthusiastic since the course started—in fact, I was never very enthusiastic in my life—so I can't possibly talk with enthusiasm about 'enthusiasm' "—what then? In that lamentable case, try to think up some subject on which you can talk with real enthusiasm. Our experience tells us that a speech which starts off: "The thing that makes me maddest. . . ." will almost inevitably be animated, forceful and interesting. Why not think of your favorite abomination, your "pettest peeve"—and talk with enthusiasm about that?

WARNING—Please, oh *please,* don't confuse *enthusiasm* with *noise.* Webster says that *enthusiasm* is: "Arden zeal, or interest; fervor." *Fervor* is "intensity of expression." Webster doesn't say a word, in that connection, about noise or yelling or stamping. What we want you to display is feeling, fervor, suppressed excitement, and we want you to do it without being noisy.

Don't expect any extended comments from your instructor after you finish your talk tonight—he will not have time for it. If you talk with stirring enthusiasm, he will say, "O.K."—which means that you scored 100. If you do not talk with enthusiasm, he will drill and drill you until you do.

Prizes Tonight, Three Pencils
The best speech prize tonight will go to the person

who spoke with the most enthusiasm; the most improvement prize will go to the person who has made the most improvement in talking with enthusiasm.

WON'T YOU PLEASE HELP ME WRITE A BOOK ON "HOW TO CONQUER FEAR AND DEVELOP SELF-CONFIDENCE"?

A Request by Dale Carnegie

I am now gathering material for a new book on "How to Conquer Fear and Develop Courage and Self-Confidence." You can help me write this book by talking about how you conquered fear. I want this new book to grow out of the experiences of our students just as the books, *How to Win Friends and Influence People* and *How to Stop Worrying and Start Living*, grew out of the experiences of earlier students in this course.

You have been given the book, *How to Stop Worrying and Start Living*. If you read this book and apply what you read, it may have a profound effect on the balance of your life for worry is the biggest personal problem facing this nation. It kills more people than do disease germs. Dr. Alexis Carrel, the famous physician and Nobel prize-winner in medicine, said, "Business men who do not know how to fight worry, die young."

So reading this book may easily bring you peace of mind and also add years to your life.

You will be requested at the twelfth session of this course — three weeks from tonight — to talk about "How I Conquered Worry" or "How I Conquered Fear."

98

Tell us about how you conquered worry after reading this new book or how you conquered worry at any time during your life. Do not begin by talking about how terrible worry is. Everybody knows that. Don't preach. Don't make a lot of general statements. Begin the very first sentence of your speech by talking about yourself and your worry problems. Begin something like this: "I worried so much I got stomach ulcers five years ago." A statement like that gets attention. It makes us want to hear more.

In the book, *How to Stop Worrying and Start Living*, you will find scores of prize-winning talks by students of this course on "How I Conquered Worry." Read them. They will show you what kinds of talks win prizes at the twelfth session.

So if you make a prize-winning talk at the twelfth session on how you conquered either fear or worry, please send me a copy of your talk to this address:

Dale Carnegie

27 Wendover Road

Forest Hills, New York

After reading your prize-winning talk, I may want to use it in either a newspaper column or in my book on *fear*. If I do use your story in the book, you will be given ten dollars and a copy of the book. If I use it in a newspaper column, you will be given an autographed copy of *How to Win Friends and Influence People*.

No student's talk, however, will be put in print without first securing his written permission.

Let me warn you that I cannot use any additional illustrations of how students conquered fear by joining this course and learning to speak in public. I now

99

have hundreds of those in my files. However, I do need additional stories of how students conquered fear and developed courage and self-confidence before taking this course.

—DALE CARNEGIE

You Should Live This Assignment

Will you begin this week to apply the "Twelve Ways to Win People to Your Way of Thinking" in *How to Win Friends and Influence People?*

"All the principles?" you ask. No, not all. Perhaps one group. Perhaps better, just one principle—the rule you break most often.

Apply this principle—see how easy it is to apply—how marvelously it produces good results!

You will be called on to speak in Session No. 10 ("How to Win People to Your Way of Thinking and How to Get Enthusiastic Cooperation") on how you applied one or more of these rules and how they worked. Please begin now to live your subject, which is the best way to prepare for that speech.

Talks, Prizes and Reading Assignment
Session Number Nine

Talks:

6:00 to 8:00 p.m. session—30 to 120 seconds—Burlesque talks.

8:00 to 10:40 p.m. session—Two talks: the first, 15 to 30 seconds—a pep talk; and the second, 2 minutes—talk on how you displayed enthusiasm and what happened.

Prizes:

8:00 to 10:40 p.m. session—Best speech, most improvement and special award pencils.

100

Reading Assignment:

In preparation for Session No. 9, please read in *Public Speaking and Influencing Men in Business:*

Chapter VI — "Essential Elements in Successful Speaking"—Pages 167 through 189.

Please review the booklet, *How One Idea Multiplied My Income and Happiness,* by Frank Bettger, which was given to you at Session No. 5.

Please read in *How to Stop Worrying and Start Living,* pages 167 through 179.

SESSION No. 10

Correct Pronunciation
   Contest ....6:00 to 8:00 p.m.
How to Win People to Your Way of
   Thinking and How to Get Enthusiastic
   Cooperation ....8:00 to 10:40 p.m.

Date..

Instructor..

Correct Pronunciation Contest—
6:00 to 8:00 p.m.

Two features tonight—a talk and a contest.

First, a 60-second talk by each member of the group. As you speak tonight, your audience will encourage you and help you to put a little life and expression into your talks. If you pull a "dead pan," your audience will make faces at you until you come alive and radiate a little facial expression of some kind: a smile, a scowl, an earnest expression—whatever fits the mood of your talk.

A topic? Anything that interests you. Want a suggestion? See if you like any of these:

1. Imagine you are facing a group of boys who are being graduated from high school. They are planning to go into business. Should they go through college first? Are four years in college worth, to a man going into business, the time and money which they cost? These boys have asked you for your advice. Give it to them!

2. Imagine that a taxpayers' association has invited you to talk on what you think about the way the taxpayers' money is spent.

102

3. Imagine that your local Rotary Club has invited you to speak on what will happen to business in the next year? Where are we headed? Why do you think so?

4. Should schools and colleges put more stress on studying and less on football?

5. Should high schools pay more attention to preparing boys and girls for life and less to preparing them to pass college examinations?

6. Are parents to blame for juvenile delinquency? If so, what can be done to reform *parents?*

7. Who will win the pennant in the . . . . League— and why?

Can you make a complete, well-rounded speech in 60 seconds? Of course you can! Here is your chance to demonstrate that fact.

And Now for the Contest

When this round of speeches is finished, you will get a test to see what you know about correct pronunciation.

Why do we give you this test?

Because, as a speaker, it is important for you to express yourself with clear, vivid words and to pronounce according to the accepted canons.

Dr. Charles W. Eliot, after he had been president of Harvard for a third of a century, declared, "I recognize but one mental acquisition as a necessary part of the education of a lady or gentleman, namely, an accurate and refined use of the mother tongue."

This contest tonight will be a pronunciation test. It will be run like an old-fashioned spelling bee.

For this test, the class will be split, by the director, into two groups and lined up in two rows, as in a spelling bee.

Each contestant will be given a list containing words often mispronounced.

If You Miss, You're Out!

The words will be given out to the contestants, one to one side and then one to the other side. When a student misses, he must sit down. The director will give the correct pronunciation of the word mispronounced and then call the next number. The team which first has fewer than five contestants left standing is the loser of the team contest—the team with five or more still standing is the winner. The contest will be continued until only two contestants are left. Then these two will battle it out for the individual championship, on this basis: When one misses, the remaining contestant will be given a word to pronounce. If his answer is correct, he is declared the champion. If he misses, the contest continues until one man misses and the other then answers correctly.

This contest is not only a test of your ability to pronounce; it is also a test of your sportsmanship. Be a good loser. Maybe you will be knocked out by the only word on the list that you don't know how to pronounce. All right—what difference will it make a hundred years from now! Nobody on earth knows all the answers. Remember, only one can win. So don't let it distress you if you are one of the losers. (In fact, Dale Carnegie admits that he probably couldn't pass this test himself.)

Our authority for all pronunciations is Webster's Unabridged Dictionary. We have tried to give only

104

words for which one, and only one, pronunciation is authorized.

Each group member will, after the contest ends, be given a sheet which contains the correct answers for this contest so that he may take it home and study it.

If Watching the Bee Bores You—Make a Speech!

If, after you are knocked out of the contest, you don't want to watch the remainder of the battle, get a few other losers together, go to another part of the room and start an informal public speaking practice session.

What Do You Mean—Correct Pronunciation?

What is correct pronunciation? That depends. What would probably be regarded as the correct pronunciation of the words *hog* and *marriage* in Kansas City might not be acceptable in Boston; and what is acceptable in Boston might sound strange to an Oxford graduate.

The dictionaries themselves sharply disagree as to what is correct pronunciation. The dictionaries attempt to do only one thing: to record the pronunciation used by a majority of the educated and cultivated people. In general, good pronunciation is pronunciation that conveys your meaning and does not call attention to itself, either because it is crude and disagreeable to the ear or because it is too, too, too "perfect." For example, to say *jist* and *git* and *ketch* is offensive to many people and so is the pronunciation *bath* with the *a* sounded as the *a* in *arm*—one is slipshod; the other sounds affected to most people.

If you desire to improve your pronunciation and English usage in public speaking, then first improve

105

them in your private conversation. When you are talking to an audience, you haven't time to give a thought to pronunciation and the rules of grammar. Good English should be as natural to you as breathing.

How to Win People to Your Way of Thinking and How to Get Enthusiastic Cooperation— 8:00 to 10:40 p.m.

Your speech tonight should be among your best speeches. Why? Because it will come out of your experiences in dealing with people. If you have, as we requested, used some of these human relations rules, you will have some real human interest illustrations. Your talk will be full of word pictures. You will have an excellent opportunity to compare right ways of dealing with people with wrong ways of dealing with people. These are the things that will make your speech vital and interesting to your audience.

By this time, you will have finished reading Part Three in *How to Win Friends and Influence People*— "Twelve Ways to Win People to Your Way of Thinking."

We eagerly hope that you have been trying out some of these principles and that you will come to this session prepared to talk about your experiences in using them.

Why not take just one principle and try it out all this week in preparation for your speech? Try it out at your office or in the shop. Try it out at home. Try it out in your social group. Talk over the rule with a number of other persons—some who use this rule successfully, some who use it unsuccessfully and some who don't use it at all. Then come to the class prepared to give a two-minute talk on your experiences in making the rule work. Be sure to tell (a) how you used the rule, (b) the results you secured and (c) what your listeners can learn from your experience.

The three students who make the best talks on the application of these rules will receive copies of The Reader's Digest Anthology, *Getting the Most Out of Life.* Vote for three.

You Get Criticism Charts

Tonight you will be given two charts containing suggestions for improvement. These charts, prepared by Dale Carnegie, ask questions about many phases of your talk. One will be marked by one class director and the other, by another. (They may prefer to take the charts home in order to mark them more carefully. In that case, the charts will be returned to you next week.)

These markings will indicate both the strong points and the weak features of your performance. They will be a permanent record of the impression your talk made tonight. Study these charts carefully and preserve them for future reference. Act upon the suggestions they contain!

One experienced speaker, who took this course recently, usually studies these charts before he makes any talks in public.

Talks, Prizes and Reading Assignment
Session Number Ten

Talks:

6:00 to 8:00 p.m. session—60 seconds—Talk on anything that interests you.

8:00 to 10:40 p.m. session — 2 minutes — Talk based on your experience in using the rules for winning people to your way of thinking.

Prizes:

8:00 to 10:40 p.m. session—Copies of the book, *Getting the Most Out of Life,* for the three winning talks. No one is eligible for these prizes who did not talk about how he or somebody used some of the rules for "winning people to your way of thinking."

Reading Assignment:

In preparation for Session No. 10, please read in *Public Speaking and Influencing Men in Business:*

Chapter VII—"The Secret of Good Delivery"— Page 193 through 221.

Don't forget "Speech Building."

Please read in *How to Stop Worrying and Start Living,* pages 180 through 193.

Speech of Introduction
  Contest ....6:00 to 8:00 p.m.

Crashing Through ....8:00 to 10:40 p.m.

Date...

Instructor..

Speech of Introduction Contest—
6:00 to 8:00 p.m.

You will be called upon this evening to introduce somebody to the class: Al Capone, Columbus, Demosthenes—pick anybody, alive or dead.

What do you say when you are called on to introduce somebody? You need to know only a few rules in order to make a good speech of introduction.

Remember, the purpose of a speech of introduction is:

(a) To tell the audience what the speaker is going to talk about; and to arouse a desire to hear his speech.

(b) To tell the audience who the speaker is and why he is qualified to talk on his subject.

Hence, the formula for a speech of introduction is: "1. Subject. 2. Speaker."

Try to Follow These Rules

Here are the rules you should follow to make an effective speech of introduction:

Rule 1. Make your speech of introduction brief. It should be as brief and condensed as a telegram—*sixty seconds ought to be enough.*

Audiences love short speeches of introduction. For example, on November 23, 1937, Dale Carnegie addressed an audience of 3,844 people in Constitution Hall in Washington, D. C. Before Dale Carnegie spoke, the manager of the lecture program, Jesse H. Knight, had to tell the audience about coming attractions and urge them to buy tickets for the entire series. He was then going to introduce Dr. H. C. Byrd, the president of the University of Maryland, who, in turn, was to introduce Dale Carnegie. Mr. Carnegie expected that five minutes would be consumed by these preliminaries, but he had a delightful surprise. The manager of the lecture series took about one minute and then introduced Dr. Byrd, who stood up and said something like this: "Most of you have read Mr. Carnegie's book. You already know who he is and you know that he is going to talk about 'How to Win Friends and Influence People.' I know you want to hear him instead of me, so here he is."

Mr. Carnegie began his talk by saying, "Ladies and gentlemen, you have just witnessed an historic occasion! Probably never before in the history of America have there ever been two such short speeches of introduction." The audience responded with enthusiastic applause.

So remember, if you make your speech of introduction short, you will be popular with both the audience and the speaker you introduce.

What to Say About the Speaker's Subject

Rule 2. Announce briefly the subject the speaker is going to discuss. If desirable, show why the subject is vital to the listeners' interests.

For example, if you were introducing an accountant who was going to speak on "Why So Many Casualties in Business?" you might begin your speech of introduction by saying, "Our speaker today is going to tell us what causes so many business casualties. Should that subject interest you business men? Well, I received a letter this week from Dun & Bradstreet" (hold the letter up so the audience can see it) "which reads: 'Of all new concerns starting in business in any one year, about 65% will fail to reach a sixth birthday.' So if we pay attention to this talk, we may save ourselves thousands of dollars. Yes, it may even save some of us from financial disaster."

Rule 3. Give some facts about the speaker.

Remember, we said give *facts*—not vague, meaningless generalities, but FACTS! Don't say he is "one of our best-known speakers," that he "has spoken to large and appreciative audiences," that he is "well qualified to talk on this subject." Such phrases are dull, trite, unconvincing. Give facts which *prove* he is equipped to discuss his subject. What has the speaker done? What position does he hold? What has he written? Why is he qualified to talk on this subject?

Suppose you are introducing a Mr. C. A. Jones, who is going to speak on "Why So Many Casualties in Business?" After announcing the subject, you might say, "Mr. C. A. Jones can speak with authority on this subject of business failures because he is the top man of C. A. Jones and Company, an accounting concern which employs 231 people, 37 of them certified public accountants. Mr. Jones himself is a C.P.A. He has been studying business problems since 1912. He is the author of the book, *Principles and Practices of Accounting.*"

Statements like these demand attention and respect. They are facts, not opinions. They are definite, not

111

vague. Most of those statements couldn't possibly be made about anyone else on earth except C. A. Jones.

The Bigger the Speaker, the Smaller the Introduction

The better known a speaker is, the less you need to say about him. The President of the United States, for example, is usually introduced in five words: "Ladies and gentlemen, the President." Only little men need big build-ups. You will sometimes find a long inscription on the tomb of a little known man; but the marble casket containing the body of George Washington at Mount Vernon bears only one word: *Washington*. The marble casket in Napoleon's tomb bears only one word: *Napoleon*. The statue of Robert E. Lee in Richmond bears only one word: *Lee*. To repeat: The bigger the man, the less you need to say about him.

Rule 4. Announce the speaker's name clearly. Give it so clearly that it couldn't possibly be misunderstood by a weak-minded chambermaid with a punctured drum in her left ear.

If the name is hard to understand, be sure to enunciate each syllable distinctly. If the speaker's name is Richens, don't mumble it and leave people wondering whether it is Hitchens or Dickens. Pronounce it in clear-cut syllables: "Rich-ens."

Be Modest, Be Modest!

Rule 5. Don't try to show off. Don't try to impress the audience with your ability or your importance.

Dale Carnegie was once introduced to an audience by a teacher of vocabulary building. This teacher was eager to impress the audience with his knowledge of big words. In what should have been a simple speech of introduction, he used several words that most of his hearers couldn't even understand. The result? The audience felt that he was trying to high-hat them, trying to show off, trying to demonstrate his mental superiority. Probably people smiled inwardly at his ridiculous exhibition. They probably pitied him as an egotistical fool. Others obviously resented him.

Take another case: A United States senator once introduced Franklin D. Roosevelt to a radio audience. Instead of following the usual form, this senator went on and on about himself and his state and its traditions. He knew better because he paused to say, in the middle of his talk, "I realize you didn't tune in to hear me. You want to hear the President, but I just want to assure the President that the state of . . . . is behind him, just as it has always been behind all forward-looking men and movements, and . . . .," and on and on he went, and on and on and on—for four full minutes. That wordy windbag should have spoken for four seconds, not four minutes.

Rule 6. Restrain the impulse to turn to the speaker when you announce his name—continue looking at the audience when you say, "I introduce Mr. Blank."

A chairman, introducing a speaker, often turns to the speaker when he says, "I introduce Mr. Blank." Don't do that. Mr. Blank certainly knows his own name, but the audience may be in some doubt. Besides, if you turn to look at Mr. Blank, your voice may not carry to the audience. So continue to face the audience while saying, "And here is Mr. Blank."

Then Make Your Exit—Fast

Rule 7. Leave the platform immediately. After you have announced the speaker's name, turn to him, bow slightly and say, in a conversational tone, "Mr. Blank." Then depart—rapidly and inconspicuously!

113

Don't, if you can avoid it, sit facing the audience after you have introduced the speaker. Why? Bad taste. Egotistical. If you continue to sit facing the audience, you demonstrate that you want to show off, just as the noblemen did in Shakespeare's time when they bought tickets to sit on the stage in order to be seen with the actors.

To sit on the platform while another man is speaking is grossly unfair to him. You can't possibly keep from moving while he talks. You are bound to move a hand or a foot occasionally, or cross your legs. Remember, every time you make the slightest movement, the audience may look at you and cease paying attention to Mr. Blank's speech. So be a good sport; and, after you introduce Mr. Blank, get off the platform and sit down modestly among the listeners, where you belong.

Here Are the Rules in Brief

To sum up:

Rule 1.   Make your speech of introduction brief.

Rule 2.   Comment briefly on the subject; and, if desirable, show why it should be interesting to the listeners.

Rule 3.   Give *facts* about the speaker.

Rule 4.   Announce the speaker's name clearly.

Rule 5.   Don't try to show off.

Rule 6.   Don't turn to the speaker when you announce his name.

Rule 7.   Leave the platform immediately.

Here's a suggestion to go with the rules: Make your talks of introduction enthusiastic. Be animated. Be alive. Make your introduction sparkle. Many speakers say to themselves, "Oh, this is just a speech of intro-

114

duction—why get worked up over it?" That is the wrong attitude. You owe it to the man you are introducing and to your audience to put a lot of zip into your talk. Act as though it was a real privilege to introduce this speaker—feel happy about it—talk with real enthusiasm.

Here We Go in the Contest!

Now that you know how to make a speech of introduction, you are going to make such a speech in a contest with your other class members. The class director will keep score.

In making the speech of introduction, you are to follow closely the seven rules given above. You will be given precisely 60 seconds to make this speech.

Whom should you introduce? It does not matter, so long as it is somebody about whom you *know the facts.*

Remember, Rule 3 requires you to state facts—FACTS. Introduce your father or your brother or your sister, or your best friend or anybody—so long as you can give the facts that qualify him or her to talk on the subject chosen. Of course, you will probably have to *imagine* the subject—but *don't imagine the facts!*

In case only one person makes a perfect score, or in case one person scores more points than anyone else, he will be declared the champion. In case of a tie, the class will have to decide by a show of hands which of those tied made the best speech of introduction.

Your director will return your score sheet to you after the contest is run off. If you didn't make a perfect score, study the sheet to see which rules you violated. You will be given a second chance tonight to make a speech of introduction—and this time you should do it perfectly.

In the second round of speeches, each student will be asked to introduce the person sitting at his right. You will be allowed two and a half minutes to get facts about the person whom you are to introduce and about a topic on which he might talk. Obviously, the student on your left will introduce you. An additional two and a half minutes will be allowed for you to give information to him.

Your director will expect you to make a perfect score on your second speech of introduction. Please don't disappoint him.

Crashing Through—8:00 to 10:40 p.m.

Expect some surprises tonight. The instructor will put you through some unusual stunts—stunts that will jar you out of your shell and give you a new freedom and a new ease.

You will be drilled tonight to project your voice in a way which will give you greater command over an audience. You will learn how to make your language live and give your talks those high spots of emphasis that will make them more impressive. You will learn how to control the flow of your language so that you will be able to "change your pace" and thus to avoid monotony. You will learn how to make your body go to work with your voice and your brain so that you will find it easier to gesture.

When you finish this session, you will be more sure of yourself as a speaker and you will have had a wonderful evening!

You do not need to prepare a speech for this session.

116

You Get Self-Analysis Charts

Every class member will be given tonight a copy of a self-analysis chart. This chart discusses different aspects of one's personality. You are urged to take this self-rating personality chart home and carefully rate yourself. No one else need see it—it is for your own personal use. Next week you will receive a sheet containing the correct answers.

Get Ready for Your Class Song

At the close of the session tonight your class director will appoint someone to write the words for a class song, to be sung by the class at the commencement exercises.

Are You Prepared for Session Twelve?

Don't forget that you will talk at Session No. 12 next week on how you conquered fear, how you developed self-confidence or how you learned not to worry. Be sure you put into practice one or more of the rules Dale Carnegie suggests in the book, *How to Stop Worrying and Start Living*—and be sure to report on the result of your experiment. If you do, you are almost certain to make a good speech.

Talks, Prizes and Reading Assignment
Session Number Eleven

Talks:

6:00 to 8:00 p.m. session—60 seconds each—Two speeches of introduction.

8:00 to 10:40 p.m. session—No speech to prepare.

Prizes:

8:00 to 10:40 p.m. session—Special award pencil

117

to the man who gave the most outstanding performance in the crashing through session—unless he has already won this prize, in which case it will go to the person who had the second largest number of votes.

Reading Assignment:

In preparation for Session No. 11, please read in *Public Speaking and Influencing Men in Business:*
Chapter VIII—"Platform Presence and Personality"—Pages 225 through 257.

Although the pronunciation contest has been conducted, please do not forget the "Speech Building" sections at the end of each of the remaining chapters assigned in *Public Speaking and Influencing Men in Business.*

Please read in *How to Stop Worrying and Start Living,* pages 194 through 213.

SESSION No. 12

Impromptu Speaking ....6:00 to 8:00 p.m.

How to Conquer Fear and
   Worry ....8:00 to 10:40 p.m.

Date...

Instructor..

Impromptu Speaking—6:00 to 8:00 p.m.

You can relax and enjoy your dinner tonight because your task for this session will be easy. You will
speak impromptu. Four minutes before your talk, your
class director will hand you a slip of paper on which
you will find written a topic or several topics.

The director knows that success in public speaking
depends more on the choice of material than upon extraordinary ability, so he will give you a subject that
fits your knowledge, interest and experience.

For example, if you are a doctor, he may hand you
the topic, "Do you believe we should have socialized
medicine? Give reasons." If you are an accountant,
you may be asked to give your views on whether or
not our tax laws need revising and to what extent.
A life insurance salesman might be given the topic,
"Why is 90% of life insurance sold by 10% of the
salesmen?" A parent might be asked to discuss the
question of whether it is better for a mother to hire a
nurse to take care of her children or to take entire
care of them herself. A stenographer might be handed
the topic, "Do women in business have to work harder
to succeed than men? If so, why?"

You will be allowed two minutes for this impromptu talk.

119

How to Conquer Fear and Worry—
8:00 to 10:40 p.m.

You were given, when you enrolled, Dale Carnegie's book, *How to Stop Worrying and Start Living.* You have been assigned chapters to read in this book each week. You have been urged to apply the rules to your own life—in preparation for your talk tonight.

Talk tonight about your own experiences with these rules—how you tried them and how they worked— or didn't work! Or, tell us some of your experiences in conquering fear and developing self-confidence.

Do *NOT* begin your talk with such general statements as: "Worry is a terrible thing. It destroys your health. It never got anybody anything." Such an opening is trite and dull. Instead, begin your speech tonight by talking about yourself. Make some such statement as this: "I was so worried five years ago that I had stomach ulcers." (In other words, try to begin your opening sentence with the word "I" and talk about your own experiences in conquering worry. If you want to do any preaching about worry, do it briefly at the end of your speech, not at the beginning.)

Do not use the magic formula at this session. Let us repeat: The magic formula is used only when you are asking the audience to *do* something. Tonight you will not ask your listeners to do anything—you will merely tell them of your experience in curing yourself of worrying—or in overcoming fear and developing self-confidence.

Tonight we suggest that you use a new and easy formula. It's a formula that you can use in writing a play, novel, short story or a motion picture scenario. This formula was given to Dale Carnegie by Howard Lindsay, co-author of "Life With Father," a play that

120

took in over $10,000,000 and ran in New York for over eight years. It broke all records in the American Theatre. Howard Lindsay says that there are three steps in writing a play:

Step I—Make the audience like the hero.

Step II —Get him into trouble.

Step III—Get him out of trouble.

See how easy it is to follow these steps in your worry talk tonight.

Step I—You are the hero in your talk. You can make your audience like you by liking them. Say to yourself before you start your talk, "I like these people. I am glad to be associated with them in this educational enterprise." Begin your talk with a friendly feeling in your heart.

Step II—Get yourself into trouble in your first sentence: "I was so worried five years ago I had stomach ulcers."

Then devote the rest of the talk telling about how you conquered worry. That will automatically take care of Step III, which is getting yourself out of trouble.

End your talk tonight by telling your class members what they can learn from your experience. Almost any talk is interesting when a man tells what life has taught him. Every sentence of your talk tonight should be as conversational as it would be if you were talking to a person across the dinner table.

Of course, if you haven't made any progress conquering fear or worry, you can't talk about it—but maybe you can tell some experience you or someone else has had with fear or worry. Or, talk about any subject you please.

121

Three Book Prizes Tonight

Three prizes will be awarded tonight for the best talks on "How I Conquered Fear" or "How I Conquered Worry." Everyone is eligible.

Vote for three people tonight.

The three prizes for tonight will be autographed copies of Dale Carnegie's book, *Biographical Round-up*. These books will not be given the prize winners tonight. They will be mailed to the winners from New York. Please send a copy of your prize winning talks on conquering fear or worry to Dale Carnegie, 27 Wendover Road, Forest Hills, N. Y. Please be sure to say that this speech won a prize at the twelfth session of Class Number . . . Please include, of course, your name and address *and also the name of the sponsor in your territory.*

May We Have Your Help Again?

Were you one of those who gave us, five or six weeks ago, the names and addresses of some of your friends who might be interested in taking the Dale Carnegie Course? If so, we are grateful to you. Could you now give us some additional names?

If you did not give us names when we asked for them previously, could you do so now?

As we stated before, we shall be glad if you will give us the names only of people with whom you have talked about the course—people who you have some reason to believe are really interested. That is, don't give us names of people who, in your opinion, *ought* to take the course unless you know that they are at least a little interested.

We shall be glad to use your name in writing to these people, but shall not do so without your written permission. The people whose names you give us will be invited to the next opening meeting.

Aides Will Be Named for Next Week

Your class director will name one or more students tonight to serve as acting class directors in the conference room session next week. These men will thus have a week to study the rules and prepare themselves to act as aides. (See page 136).

Gather Some Ammunition

You will be asked, in the conference session, to talk for 60 seconds on what should be done to improve the city or town in which you live. You will be required to support your point and reason with an incident, statistics, expert testimony or an exhibit. So please decide on your subject as soon as practicable and start to gather material.

Talks, Prizes and Reading Assignment
Session Number Twelve

Talks:

6:00 to 8:00 p.m. session—2 minutes—Impromptu talk.

8:00 to 10:40 p.m. session—2 minutes—Talk on how you conquered fear or worry.

Prizes:

8:00 to 10:40 p.m. session—Copies of the book, *Biographical Roundup,* to the three students who made the best talks on "How I Conquered Fear" or "How I Conquered Worry." (The prize books will be mailed upon receipt, by Dale Carnegie, of a written copy of each talk.)

Reading Assignment:

In preparation for Session No. 12, please read in *Public Speaking and Influencing Men in Business:*

    Chapter X—"Capturing Your Audience at Once" Pages 295 through 321.

Please read in *How to Stop Worrying and Start Living*, pages 214 through 224.

Solving Your Personal Speaking
Problems ....6:00 to 8:00 p.m.

How to Save Time and Get Far Better
Results in Conferences.........8:00 to 10:40 p.m.

Date..

Instructor...

Solving Your Personal Speaking Problems— 6:00 to 8:00 p.m.

Tonight you will take part in a laboratory session. You will, in this session, take stock of what you have already accomplished in the course; look ahead to what you still wish to gain; discuss your own speaking and human relations problems and get the advice and guidance of the other members of your class.

Don't bother about preparing a talk for this session. Just do a little thinking about your speaking and human relations problems—then, in the class session, discuss these problems frankly and honestly and ask for help.

Here is how this session will be handled:

You will be called in the usual way and will talk for 60 seconds on your problems. At the end of this talk, you will ask for solutions. The director will ask which students can offer suggestions that may help. As soon as people put up their hands, *you* will give the nod to the one you would like to hear from. The person thus selected will be entitled to 60 seconds of time in an effort to make suggestions that will help. If no one volunteers or if the same persons volunteer over and over, the director will call on some member of the class to offer suggestions. So you have to stay wide awake in this session because at any time you may be the one called on to talk.

Can fellow students, many of whom have not studied public speaking or human relations any longer than you have, be of any help to you in solving your speaking and human relations problems? You will be astonished—and helped and stimulated—by the suggestions you will get.

Begin Thinking About Candidates for the Position of Class Directors

Two weeks from tonight you will do some voting that is of vital interest to future classes. You will vote for the four people in your class who, you feel, are best fitted to serve as class directors next semester. Please begin thinking about this. Consider first what qualities a class director should have. Surely by now you know the qualities you like in a director. Then consider which four people in the class are most bountifully supplied with these qualities.

The men and women selected will be given the opportunity to attend the directors school.

Mr. Carnegie and all those associated with him will greatly appreciate it if you will give this point deep consideration.

How to Save Time and Get Far Better Results in Conferences—8:00 to 10:40 p.m.

Most of you who take this course aspire to forge ahead and win a position of leadership in society, in politics, in your business or profession. If you weren't ambitious, you wouldn't be in this class. In order to become a leader, you must be able to take an active

126

part in conferences and discussions and to lead meetings.

Some students say, "I'm not interested—I never take part in a conference."

What nonsense! Everybody who can *speak* takes part almost daily in conferences. When a husband and wife take up the question of what show to see tonight, they are engaging in a conference. When a mother talks with her children about whether or not they ought to play with tough little Johnny Blank down the street, they are participants in a conference. What is a committee meeting but a conference—and what is the chairman but a conference leader!

Because we all engage in conferences daily, this session is intensely practical. In it you learn:

a. How to talk effectively in a conference.

b. How to take an active part in a conference.

c. How to lead a conference.

What You Do in This Session

Here is the program for this session:

1. Brief opening talk by instructor.
2. Explanation of PRES formula by instructor.
3. "Town meeting" talks.
4. Drill on "trouble shooting" questions and their uses.
5. Demonstration of a conference.
6. Recess.
7. Group conferences.

You Already Know This Formula

The formula which you will use for your "town meeting" talk and, with obvious modification, in your

conference room talks is called the PRES formula—
that is, point, reason, example, *so what*. These, of
course, are the last four steps of the magic formula.
In your "town meeting" talk, please use this formula.

After your instructor has drilled your class briefly
in the PRES formula, he will resolve the session into
an old-fashioned "town meeting." Each student will
talk for 60 seconds on the subject, "How We Can Improve Our City." ("Our city" means, not the city in
which the class is held, but rather the city or town in
which the speaker lives.) The instructor will throw
the meeting open by asking the question, "How can
we improve our city—who has a suggestion?" After
all volunteer speakers have made their suggestions,
the instructor will call on those who have not spoken.

Don't feel that you have to suggest a different improvement from those already suggested. It is all right
if you add your support to some suggestion which has
already been made.

This part of the session will be even livelier if some
of the students will speak in opposition to some of the
suggestions made. That is, if one student suggests the
building of an overhead highway, another might op-
pose this on the ground that the city could not afford
it. Remember, however, if you speak in rebuttal, you
are entitled to make no other speech in the "town-
meeting"—that is, you will not be allowed to speak
more than once in the "town meeting."

Your "town meeting" talk is to be a prepared
speech —please prepare it carefully. Especially, support your point and reason with an incident, statistics,
expert testimony or an exhibit.

For instance, a speaker in Chicago might say, "My
point is: I want you to petition the mayor to instruct

the police department to conduct a campaign against the unnecessary blowing of automobile horns. My reason is: Such a campaign really produces results." The speaker has now made a claim—that such a campaign produces results. If he expects anyone to believe his claim, he must support it with some evidence. To do so, he might say, "Take, for example, what La Guardia did when he was mayor of New York. He conducted an anti-noise campaign that not only produced immediate results, but which has continued to produce results. How do I know? Why, when I was in New York the other day, there was far less unnecessary blowing of automobile horns in that city than in Chicago."

In general, your example should support your point and reason. Many students will use their example merely to prove that something is wrong—not that their proposed remedy will work. For example, a student will say, "What this town needs is an underground parking place. The parking situation in this city is terrible. This morning, when I came to work, I drove about a mile across 36th and 37th and 38th Streets and was late at work. So let's petition the mayor to build an underground parking place." What has this student done? He has supported his claim that the parking situation is bad. He has not supported his claim that an underground parking place would solve the city's parking problem.

It is quite all right to use an example to prove that a situation exists that needs remedying, but you should also—if possible—give some evidence to support your claim that your suggested remedy will work. For example, in the case cited above, you might say, "Underground parking would really solve our problem. Look at what it has done in San Francisco," etc., etc. In other words, you would be giving some evidence that your proposed remedy would really cure the ill.

So, after you have picked your example, ask yourself: "Does my example really prove that my suggested remedy will work?" If not, please try to get an example that will support your point and reason.

Note that it is not *always* necessary to prove that your suggested remedy will work. For example: Point: "Go to bed at the usual time, but get up an hour earlier;" reason, "to give you an hour extra for reading." Obviously you do not need evidence to prove that, if a man goes to bed at the usual time and gets up an hour earlier, he gains an hour!

Remember, your talk will get no praise from the instructor unless, in some effective way, you support your reason where it is desirable.

Please Memorize These Four Questions

The instructor's next job tonight is to be sure that the class members know the four questions to ask in any problem-solving conference—questions that will give "trouble shooting" conferences light and clarity, purpose and direction, speed and action. Please memorize these four questions and use them in discussions at the office, in the home, and whenever you are trying to solve problems.

Here are the "trouble shooting" questions:

1. *What is the trouble?*
2. *What are the causes of the trouble?*
3. *What are the possible solutions?*
4. *What is the best possible solution?*

Let's see how you can use these four questions in practice. Suppose, for example, that we are partners in a retail store, and we are holding a conference to see how we can increase our profits. So we ask:

Step 1. *What is the trouble?*

Prices too high? Lack of appeal in advertising? Delivery service slow? Credit practices bad? No, let's suppose the discussion reveals that our chief trouble is disinterested and discourteous clerks.

Step 2. *What are the causes of the trouble?*

Why are the clerks disinterested and discourteous? Is it because no one has ever made them *want* to be interested and courteous?

Or are they overworked? Fatigue often breeds discourtesy. Even Lord Chesterfield was probably a bit grouchy when he was exhausted.

The clerks may feel that they are underpaid—and resent it, and so may not want to be interested in their work.

Step 3. *What are all the possible solutions?*

Here are some possible solutions:

1. We can fire the worst offenders and threaten the others.

2. We can lecture them about the necessity of courtesy and interest in their work.

3. We can give them a bonus on every sale.

4. We can point out to them that, if they develop the habit of courtesy, they themselves will profit in the following ways:

(a) Socially they will be more popular. Courtesy will help the girls get dates and maybe get and hold husbands.

(b) Being courteous will be more fun.

(c) Since discourtesy is the biggest problem in

retail stores, the courteous clerk should get ahead more rapidly.

(d) Courtesy and taking an interest in their work will relieve boredom and fatigue, and so make them feel more refreshed after they go home.

Step 4. What is the best possible solution?

We have discussed four possible solutions for the problem of disinterested clerks. A combination of two of these solutions will give us the best possible solution; and you don't have to be a Ph.D. from Harvard to pick out the two we mean.

How to Keep a Conference on the Track

Tonight, your instructor, after he has drilled the class on the four questions, will pin on the wall four cards on which are printed the four questions we have been discussing: "What is the trouble? What are the causes of the trouble?" and so on. You will probably refer to them many times tonight.

If You Are Wise, You Will Learn These Rules

Because you will certainly take part in a conference tonight and because you will perhaps serve also as a conference leader, you ought to know the rules for leading a conference and the rules for taking part in a conference. These rules follow. Please read them over again and again until you are quite familiar with them. If you take part in many conferences in your business or professional life, you ought to memorize them word for word.

Rules on How to Lead a Conference:

Dale Carnegie recommends that conference leaders observe these rules:

132

1. *Open the conference with a brief statement of the problem.*

2. *Don't express your own personal ideas.* Your job is to direct and lead—not to participate in the discussion.

3. *Pay little attention to the rules of parliamentary law.*

No man in captivity knows all the complicated rules and precedents involved in parliamentary law. For instance, the decisions on points of parliamentary law which govern the United States House of Representatives are contained in eight volumes of about a thousand pages each! It would take ten years of study to master all these rules and precedents. So use your common sense—and let it go at that.

4. *Keep the conference moving.* Make it march. Short talks! Speed! Action!

5. *See that everyone participates.* Squelch the hog who tries to talk too long or too often.

6. *Keep the conference on the track.* If a man gets off the point—whang!—hit the table! Say: "The question we are discussing is so and so. Let's stick to it."

7. *Make frequent summaries.*

8. *Never go around the table and ask each person his views.* That is, don't say, "John, what do you think? Bill, what do you think? Pat, what do you think?" Instead, state the problem (or the subject) and then wait for somebody to say something on it. The only time you interfere is (a) when one person talks too much (then you politely squelch him), (b) when a person talks too little (in that case you try to draw him into the conference) and (c) when the conference gets off the track.

133

9. *When the discussion has gone far enough, summarize it.* Then call for a vote; and, if necessary, appoint a committee to see that the decision is translated into action.

Rules on How to Take Part in a Conference:

You will get more done in conferences if all participants observe these rules:

1. *Keep your talks brief.*

2. *Take up only one point at a time.* (That is, if you have three reasons for being against a proposal, don't present them one right after the other. Instead, give one reason, then give somebody else a chance, then state your second reason, and so on.)

3. *Don't talk too often;* but, on the other hand—

4. *Take an active part in the discussion.*

5. *Stick to the subject*—don't get off the track.

6. *Support every reason you give with an example or other evidence.*

7. *Don't interrupt other speakers.*

8. *Don't converse with your neighbors.*

9. *Listen attentively to all speakers.*

10. *Don't "make speeches"*—talk in an easy, conversational way.

11. *In a decision making conference, test everything you do or say by asking yourself this question: "Will it help me to win my point?"*

12. *Don't rise to speak.* Talk from your chair.

13. *Instead of making direct assertions, ask questions.*

14. *Be careful of the tones you use.* Aren't tones sometimes more important than words? You can, for

134

example, ask a question in a tone that suggests a humble seeking after truth; or you can ask it in a tone that implies that the person you are talking to is a congenital idiot. How can you get friendly tones in your voice? By first having a friendly attitude in your heart.

15. *If a speaker makes a statement with which you disagree, don't argue; but ask him why he believes as he does.* If *"why"* is asked in the proper tone, it won't arouse resentment; and it enables you to find out why the other person feels as he does. It may get you highly valuable information. Keep on asking one *"why"* after another. That will enable you to find out what cards the other player holds without disclosing your own hand. Frank Bettger, probably America's number one teacher of salesmanship, regards the word *"why"* as one of the most important words in the English language. He declares that the habit of asking *"why"* instead of arguing, has put many thousands of dollars into his bank account. So why not try *"why"* in your next conference?

Use the "How to Win Friends" Rules, Too

In addition to the rules given above, 30 of the rules set forth in *How to Win Friends and Influence People* should also govern your words and actions in a conference—whether you are a leader or merely a participant. So, before coming to class tonight, be sure to review the first 30 rules which appear at the end of this booklet.

If you follow all these 30 rules sincerely—and if you use the four problem-solving questions and the rules for conference leadership and conference participation, you will gain power, influence and prestige in almost any problem-solving conference.

Now You Will See How It Is Done

You will next take part in a demonstration of how a conference should be conducted. All class members will take part in this conference. Your instructor will act as leader. He will select a subject for discussion. This will be a problem which the class will try to solve. After stating the problem, the instructor will ask for the causes.

When the causes have been thoroughly explored, he will ask the class members to suggest possible solutions. At the end, he may take a vote as to the best possible solution; but more probably will—without recording the vote—ask each class member which solution he thinks is best.

Throughout this demonstration of a conference, the instructor will observe the rules for *leading* a conference and will insist that the class members observe the rules for *participating* in a conference. If you break a rule, he will call your attention to this infraction.

As soon as the instructor declares the demonstration at an end, the class will take the usual mid-session recess.

Now for the Small Group Conferences

Immediately after recess, class members will seat themselves in groups of eight or ten.

A class director (or some student who has been made "acting class director" for the evening) will be in charge of each group. He will not take part in the conference himself, but will see that the leader and the participants observe the rules of conference discussion.

Each group will select a leader by acclamation. The instructor will give each group the same problem.

136

Then the group leader will apply the problem-solving questions. First, he will ask, "What is the problem?" After the group members have narrowed down the problem to one which is suitable for discussion and defined it clearly, they will take up the next question, which is: "How did the problem arise?" Students should not make speeches at this point—they should merely suggest in a few words the "causes." Then they are ready for the third question: "What are the possible solutions?" At this point, the real discussion should begin. The group members will suggest their solutions and back up their suggestions with evidence —perhaps with statistics, perhaps by quoting some authority, but usually by giving an incident. (Please be sure, after you suggest a solution for the problem under discussion, that you do give some testimony to support your contentions that your suggested solution will really work. See the suggestions regarding support of point and reason under "town meeting" talks, pages 128-130.)

At the end of about 15 minutes, the instructor will declare all conferences ended and will ask the leaders of each conference to tell the entire class in one minute the results of the deliberation in his group.

New Group, New Leader, New Subject!

In order to make the ensuing conferences more interesting, the instructor will then provide a new problem, new leaders and new groups. To do this:

1. He will ask half the members of each group to "progress," as in a progressive card party.

2. He will ask each group to select a new leader.

3. He will supply each group with a problem—the same problem for each group.

Then a new conference will be held, as previously outlined.

The second conference will continue for about 15 minutes. Then the leaders will again report and the groups will again be broken up, as indicated above. These 15-minute conferences will continue until about 10:30.

In these conferences if a group member violates one of the rules for conference participation, the leader of that group should tactfully straighten him out. If the leader does not do so, it is the duty of the director or acting director to do so. If a leader violates a rule, the director or acting director should call his attention to it. The instructor will circulate from group to group to answer questions, solve problems and keep all of the conferences running at about the same rate of speed.

The instructor will close the session with a two-minute summation of what students have learned and how they can use it.

Talks, Prizes and Reading Assignment
Session Number Thirteen

Talks:

6:00 to 8:00 p.m. session—60 seconds—Informal talk on your own speaking and human relations problems.

8:00 to 10:40 p.m. session—60 seconds—Subject: "How We Can Improve Our City."
Informal conference discussions—topics assigned at session.

Prizes:

No prizes tonight.

Reading Assignment:

In preparation for Session No. 13, please read in *Public Speaking and Influencing Men in Business:*

Chapter XII—"How to Make Your Meaning Clear"—Pages 353 through 381.

Chapter XVI — "Improving Your Diction" — Pages 487 through 517.

Please read in *How to Stop Worrying and Start Living,* pages 225 through 238.

Impromptu Speaking
Contest ....6:00 to 8:00 p.m.
How to Make a Better Magic
Formula Talk ....8:00 to 10:40 p.m.

Date..

Instructor..

Impromptu Speaking Contest—
6:00 to 8:00 p.m.

Your group will hold a contest tonight to select the impromptu speech champion of your class.

Your class director will prepare the speech subjects.

He is asked to prepare for all class members subjects on which they have earned the right to speak— but have not yet spoken. For example, suppose a salesman has spoken on "How to Arouse Interest" and "How to Close the Sale"; the director might ask him to speak on "How to Arouse the Desire of Your Prospect to Own Your Goods." In this case, the speaker would be familiar with the subject and ought to be able to speak well on it. Since, by this time, your class director knows all class members well, he can give each one an appropriate subject.

The names of the class members will be written on slips and put into a hat. Four minutes before the contest is to start, the class director will pull a name out of the hat and will assign a subject to the speaker thus selected. The student will immediately start preparing his impromptu speech. At the end of two minutes, another name will be drawn and the person whose name is thus selected (who will be the second speaker) will be assigned his subject by the class director. At the end of another two minutes, a third contestant will be drawn and the first contestant will begin his impromptu speech.

Thereafter, as soon as a person has finished speaking, another contestant will be drawn and will be assigned his subject. In that way, each contestant will have approximately four minutes to prepare his speech.

When each speaker comes to the platform to speak, he will hand his subject to the class director, who will read it aloud to the listeners—so they can be sure the speaker is sticking to the assigned subject.

After all have spoken, the class members will vote by secret ballot for the person they thought made the best speech of the evening. The winner is the impromptu speech champion of the class and will be awarded a special mechanical pencil inscribed "Dale Carnegie Course—Impromptu Speech Champion."

Ponder Now—Vote Next Week

You know by now that a class director can make or break a class because he is in charge of all drill-in-speaking sessions and the first part of all regular sessions.

Please give some thought to the question of which people in your class are qualified to be directors—which people you will vote for when you ballot for director candidates next week. Pick somebody who has sincerity, enthusiasm, an eager desire to help others. Pick somebody who has studied the textbooks, somebody who can make at least a fairly good speech. Pick somebody who uses good English and who pronounces words with reasonable correctness. Pick somebody who is a leader and who has executive ability. Please think about this problem—the vote comes next week.

How to Make a Better Magic Formula Talk— 8:00 to 10:40 p.m.

You can't possibly learn in one or two sessions all you ought to know about the magic formula—so here comes the third magic formula session!

To prepare for this session, please study again the booklet, *How to Put Magic in the Magic Formula*, by Dale Carnegie. Then think out a talk in which you ask the audience to *do* something.

Your speech tonight will be just as good as its subject—and no better! So remember the rule: Pick something you have earned the right to talk about—and something you earnestly desire to "sell" to your audience.

Talk to your classmates, for instance, about something you eagerly desire them to do—to attend practice sessions or to speak for some good cause. Perhaps you can't think of anything you want the class members to do. All right, then imagine an audience and pick an idea you want to sell to that audience. (If your speech is addressed to an imaginary audience, be sure to indicate the audience you have selected before you start or in the first sentence of your speech.)

Ask Your Audience to Act

Don't make a dull, lifeless speech tonight. Make one with fire and animation and sincerity. You can do it— if you pick an explosive subject, something that fairly blows up inside you. Imagine you are talking to the city council to urge them to make Blank Street a one-way street. Imagine that you are talking

142

to the Parent Teachers Association to urge them to help get public speaking made a required subject in high school. Imagine that you are talking to the greens committee of your golf club, to urge them to fill in that pestiferous trap on the third hole. In short, pick a subject you feel deeply and that you want your audience to feel deeply — AND DO SOMETHING ABOUT!

Try especially to start with an effective *ho hum*. Remember to use one of the five ways to get an interesting *ho hum* recommended in *How to Put Magic in the Magic Formula.*.

Here they are:

1. Promise to tell the audience how they can get something they want.

2. Ask for a show of hands. (Please don't use this tonight unless you can use it effectively. If, when you ask for a show of hands, everyone present puts up his hand—or if nobody puts up his hand, it is usually a poor *ho hum*. The test is: Did it make your listeners *think?* If it did, it is usually effective. Your instructor will not accept any show-of-hands *ho hum* that is banal, silly or otherwise ineffective.)

3. Arouse suspense. ("Too difficult," you say. Imitate one of the sample *ho hums* given in the magic formula booklet and you will find it easy.)

4. State an arresting fact.

5. Begin with an illustration.

Please pick up your magic formula booklet and study these openings in detail.

Use the "Dinner Table Test"

After you have decided on your *ho hum*, give it the "dinner table test" which Dale Carnegie recom-

143

mends in *How to Put Magic in the Magic Formula*—
that is, test it by asking yourself if you could say it
naturally to a friend at the dinner table. If you can't,
then either recast it or discard it.

Usually, by changing it a little, you can make it
sound conversational. Suppose, for example, you had
decided on this as your *ho hum*: "There are more fish
in the sea than ever were caught—but you sometimes
need new bait." You would not start a conversation
with that, but you could start one by saying, "I had
an experience last night that convinced me that there
are more fish in the sea," etc.

That would be a reasonable way to start a conversation and it would be an excellent way to start
a *ho hum*.

Albert J. Beveridge, one of the all-time oratorical
greats of the United States, said in his book, *The Art
of Public Speaking,* "Let your start be conversational,
quite as though you were talking to a friend." No
better advice as to *ho hums* was ever given.

Your instructor will insist that tonight you have an
interesting *ho hum.* He will insist also that your example be relevant and that, if it is the incident type
of example, it has action. He will check up to be sure
your *so what* (a) asks your audience to do something
specific, (b) asks for some response that is within
their power to give and (c) is easy for the audience
to do.

You should work hard on this talk because tonight
you will be expected to deliver a practically perfect
magic formula talk—one that observes all the rules,
one really calculated to make the audience act.

The prizes in this part of the session are the best
speech and most improvement pencils.

Begin to Get Material for a Human Relations Talk

You will talk at the fifteenth session on how you used one or more of the "Nine Rules for Changing People Without Giving Offense or Arousing Resentment." To prepare for this session, please read Part Four, pages 221 through 253, in *How to Win Friends and Influence People*.

Then pick out one or a group of these rules and put them into practice. If you do, you are bound to turn up at the fifteenth session with a talk that boils right out of you.

Talks, Prizes and Reading Assignment
Session Number Fourteen

Talks:

6:00 to 8:00 p.m. session—No prepared talk (but a 2-minute impromptu talk for the impromptu speech championship.)

8:00 to 10:40 p.m. session — 2 minutes — Magic formula talk.

Prizes:

6:00 to 8:00 p.m. session—Impromptu speaking championship pencil.

8:00 to 10:40 p.m. session—Best speech and most improvement pencils.

Reading Assignment:

In preparation for Session No. 14, please read in *Public Speaking and Influencing Men in Business:*

Chapter XIII—"How to Be Impressive and Convincing"—Pages 385 through 415.

145

Prepared Speech Contest......6:00 to 8:00 p.m.

How to Change People Without
Giving Offense or Arousing
Resentment ....8:00 to 10:40 p.m.

Date..

Instructor..

Prepared Speech Contest—6:00 to 8:00 p.m.

Your class will hold a contest tonight to select the prepared speech champion.

Pick your topic and come to class tonight fired with a determination to give the best two-minute talk of your life. Don't let your ambition trap you into the mistake of memorizing your talk.

In spite of all our pleading, in spite of all the evidence that memorized speeches are almost always poor speeches, in spite of the fact that students have heard speaker after speaker in class sessions fail because they were trying to memorize words instead of ideas—in spite of all this—a lot of people will go into this session with a memorized speech!

The result: failure!

Just get in mind the ideas—then stand up and let the words come tumbling out, helter-skelter—just the way they do in ordinary conversation—and in effective speeches.

Oh yes—and don't forget to have an example. If it is an all-generalities talk, it is bound to be dull and uninteresting. Class members are asked not to vote (a) for any speaker who has a memorized talk or (b)

146

for any speaker whose talk does not contain an example.

The prepared speech champion will receive a special mechanical pencil inscribed "Dale Carnegie Course—Prepared Speech Champion."

The winner of last week's impromptu speech contest is not eligible to win this prize.

Class Will Nominate Class Directors

Just before the first part of the session ends, the class will vote, by secret ballot, to nominate four of its members as candidates for positions as class directors for the next semester. This is the most important vote you will cast in the entire course. Please give it serious thought. If you make a bad choice, you may wreck a future class. Your directors will not look at these votes, but will at once seal them in an envelope, together with their recommendations, and mail them to the sponsor of the course in your territory.

Don't vote for a man just because he is a "good fellow," don't vote for a man merely because he has campaigned for the job. Remember, being a class director is a difficult and important job. Try to pick men and women who will be efficient class directors and who will be a credit to your class and to the organization.

How to Change People Without Giving Offense or Arousing Resentment— 8:00 to 10:40 p.m.

"Don't get your speeches from a book," says *Modern Speaking*. "They will have all the dullness of an encyclopedia and none of its dignity." Good speeches

147

don't come out of books—they come out of lives. *Your* best speeches will come out of *your* life. They will be the story of something you have seen, done, heard, felt, LIVED!

You have now read almost all of Dale Carnegie's book, *How to Win Friends and Influence People*. If you have put into practice the rules he advocates, you must surely have had many stimulating experiences.

This session is designed to give you an opportunity to talk about one of your experiences in "Changing People Without Giving Offense or Arousing Resentment." Build a two-minute talk on your experiences in using these rules—one or a group of them. (Or, if you prefer, talk about how you used some other human relations rule.)

We want you to talk about these experiences tonight for two reasons: (1) It will help you to make a good speech and (2) it will encourage you to keep on using the rules.

Now You Get More Drill in the Magic Formula

You will do something tonight that you did not do in either of the other "How to Win Friends" sessions. In those sessions, you merely told an incident—something that had happened to you. You didn't bother with *ho hums* or *so whats*. In fact—your talk was probably just an example.

Tonight, however, we want you to use the magic formula. How?

Think out your talk in the usual way: by determining point, reason, example, *so what* and then going back and working out a *ho hum*. (Once you have your talk well in mind, you may want to combine or eliminate some of the steps or to use them in a different order, as suggested in the supplement in the magic formula booklet. However, while you are getting your talk in mind, better follow the suggestions given below—then do your eliminating and combining later.

Go ahead now and think through your talk—in this order:

1. *Point:* Use the human relations rule on which your talk is based as your point.

2. *Example:* Use the experience you had with the rule as your example.

3. *Reason:* Use a reason that is supported by your example. (Suppose you used Rule 5: "Let the other man save his face." Suppose that, as a result, you won the loyalty of an employee—then your point would be: "Let the other man save his face" and the reason would be: "because it may help you to win the loyalty of your subordinates.")

4. *So What:* Restate your point. Give specific details as to what you want the audience to do.

5. *Ho Hum:* Decide on an opening that will interest your audience—and your speech is all prepared.

Please remember to put these steps, when you deliver your talk, in the proper order of a magic formular speech.

Let's consider another example:

Suppose the rule you worked on was: "Begin with praise and honest appreciation," and suppose that, as a result of using this rule, you won the friendship of a man whose help you needed. In that case you could lay out your speech as follows:

Point: Begin with praise and honest appreciation.

Reason: Because people will cooperate with you more willingly if you do.

Example: The man in charge of our watch-repairing department is an expert workman, but a most cantankerous and uncooperative person. When people came in to have their watches regulated, he would snarl at them and complain. He was driving customers away, so something had to be done. I knew, if I went to him and told him he'd have to do better—he'd just do worse! So I used the rule—I began with sincere praise. I told him what an uncanny knack he had of regulating watches so that they would keep good time; I repeated several complimentary remarks that customers had made about him; I told him—and it's true—that we could hardly operate successfully without him. Then I tactfully suggested that he try to be more courteous to customers. Because I had begun with praise, he was willing to take suggestions. He has since shown marvelous improvement in his human relations.

So What: So, if you want to change people without giving offense or arousing resentment, use the rule: "Begin with praise and honest appreciation."

Ho Hum: I learned a rule from Dale Carnegie that is going to be worth many thousands of dollars to my company—that may be worth thousands to you.

Put this *ho hum* at the start and you have a magic formula speech based on a Dale Carnegie rule.

Let's take another case and let's begin with the example:

Example: About a third of a century ago, I was working on the Atlanta Georgian when we were stunned by the news that W. R. Hearst had bought

150

the paper. Mr. Hearst sent down almost immediately a force of men to change the paper over to the Hearst style. He sent, as publisher, Keats Speed. In the year or more I worked for Mr. Speed, I never heard him issue an order. He would ask, "Don't you think Mr. Hearst would like it this way?" or "Would it be a good idea to leave this out and put in this?"

What was the result? The men on the paper worshipped him and worked harder for him than they had ever worked before in their lives.

There's your example—how are you going to build a magic formula speech? First ask, "What is your point?" Of course the point is the rule you used—so you will ask your audience to use that rule. You will say:

Point: To get people to change willingly, ask questions instead of giving direct orders.

Now for your reason:

Reason: Because, if you do, you will have more loyal and willing employees.

Then you give the example as set forth above. Finally, you ask the audience to do what you want them to do, thus:

So What: So, if you want to change people without giving offense and arousing resentment—if you want to hold their loyalty and cooperation, use the rule that worked so well for Keats Speed: "Ask questions instead of giving direct orders."

Ho Hum: When I was a boy, it seemed to me that my parents did little but issue orders to me. It was all: "Do this and — don't do that." This technique brought out all the stubborness in me. I rarely did anything they wanted me to—willingly.

Put the steps in the proper order and you have a magic formula speech based on the rule: "Ask questions instead of giving direct orders."

You will find it interesting and stimulating to practice building magic formula talks on your experiences in using the rules for changing people.

Best speech and most improvement pencils will be awarded in this part of the session.

Talks, Prizes and Reading Assignment
Session Number Fifteen

Talks:

6:00 to 8:00 p.m. session—2 minutes—Prepared speech championship talk.

8:00 to 10:40 p.m. session — 2 minutes — Magic formula talk based on the use of one or more of the rules for changing people without giving offense or arousing resentment.

Prizes:

6:00 to 8:00 p.m. session—Prepared speech championship pencil.

8:00 to 10:40 p.m. session—Best speech and most improvement pencils.

Reading Assignment:

In preparation for Session No. 15, please read in *How to Win Friends and Influence People:*

Part IV—"Nine Ways to Change People Without Giving Offense or Arousing Resentment"—Pages 221 through 253.

SESSION No. 16

"What I Got Out of the Course"
Contest ....6:00 to 8:00 p.m.

Secrets of Successful
Speaking ....8:00 to 10:40 p.m.

Date..

Instructor..

"What I Got Out of the Course" Contest— 6:00 to 8:00 p.m.

Now for the last class contest—the contest to determine which student got the most out of the course.

This contest will be governed by the same rules as the prepared speech contest, except that you will be asked to vote, not for the person who made the best speech, but for the person who, you believe, got the most out of the course. Do you want to know how to organize this talk? It's quite simple. Just imagine that somebody had asked you these two questions:

1. Why did you take the Dale Carnegie Course?

2. What did you get out of it?

If you will answer these questions in a simple, conversational way, you will make a good speech.

Perhaps you do not want to talk on this subject. That will be quite all right. In this course, in any session, you may talk about anything you want to—but your subject should be something you have earned the right to talk about and something you earnestly desire to get across to your audience.

Remember the one great rule for this talk is: *Have an example.* Class members are asked NOT to vote

153

for any speaker who did not have an example in his talk. Don't vote for the man who rattles off a string of generalities about courage, friendship and oratory. What he should talk about is: his reasons for taking the course and his gains by doing it.

Speeches Without Examples Are Out

Please be guided accordingly in preparing your talks and in voting for the winners. Don't vote for anybody who does not answer those questions and who does not have an interesting example. If you say, "I overcame fear in this course," follow immediately by saying, "For example," etc. If you say, "I got a better job as a result of taking this course," give us an example—what was the job, just how did you get it, what did your boss say when he gave it to you?

Be specific, be concrete, answer the questions, give an example—and you will be astonished what an excellent speech you will make.

The "What I Got Out of the Course" speech champion of the class will be awarded a special mechanical pencil marked "Dale Carnegie Course—'What I Got Out of the Course' Speech Champion."

Now to Select Your Representatives

Your class will probably be represented at the commencement exercises by three speakers. One will make an impromptu speech, one a prepared speech and one will talk on "What I Got Out of the Course."

In most cities, a contest is held among representatives of all classes which are being graduated. In a few cities, the class representatives merely deliver exhibition talks.

Whatever you do in your city, you should select your three representatives by secret ballot.

154

Whom should you vote for? Not the people you like best, not the most popular members of the class, but rather the three people who, you feel, will best represent you. If your class is to compete with other classes in the commencement exercises, you will be anxious to have your class carry off the honors. Think how proud you will be if your class makes a "grand slam" and goes home with all three prizes. Therefore, vote for the best speakers. Perhaps the strongest candidates are those who won the championship contests —but not necessarily. Be guided by your judgment— vote for the best speakers.

The three students who receive the greatest number of votes in each balloting will be your representatives.

In each case, the "runner-up" qualifies as an alternate representative at the commencement exercises and will speak if, for any reason, the elected representative is unable to do so.

NOTE: *The above plan is applicable when three or more classes can be brought together for the commencement exercises.*

In case only one or two classes can be brought together, it is necessary to qualify more students to represent the class at the commencement exercises. If two classes are to meet, qualify two representatives for each contest. If your class is going to meet by itself, qualify three speakers for each contest.

Secrets of Successful Speaking—
8:00 to 10:40 p.m.

HOW YOUR TALK WILL BE JUDGED

by DALE CARNEGIE

Tonight the instructor and the members of your class are going to judge your speech by asking only one question: "What effect did it have on me?"

That is all you need to ask in judging any talk; yet, a few years ago, a college professor of public speaking wrote a book on how to judge a speech. He advocated a lot of sheer, stupid nonsense, such as judging a speech on the basis of so many points for gestures, so many points for posture, voice, emphasis, force, platform presence, facial expression, reasoning, evidence, organization, opening, closing and so on. The idea of judging a speech in that mechanical manner is not merely stupid; it is harmful and misleading. The real essence of a speech is something as difficult to describe as personality. It is as fleeting and intangible as the flame that plays over a rum omelette.

When it comes to judging a speech, I agree enthusiastically with Professor Ormond J. Drake, assistant dean of the College of Arts and Pure Science and Chairman of the Department of Speech and Dramatics, New York University. He says, "The best way to judge a speech is to sit back and try to be human; and you will then find that the best speaker is the one who affects your senses the most deeply. This means, in terms of modern psychology, the man who gained and held your attention the most completely."

Try to Get and Hold Attention

If you are able to gain and hold the complete and favorable attention of your listeners, you may have innumerable kinds of faults and nobody will care.

Mispronouncing words won't kill a speech: Lincoln mispronounced a word at Gettysburg.

Lack of gestures won't kill a speech: Lincoln used no gestures at Gettysburg.

An unattractive voice won't kill a speech: Lincoln spoke in a high, thin tenor voice at Gettysburg.

Being dressed like a scarecrow won't kill a speech: When Lincoln spoke against the repeal of the Missouri Compromise on October 3, 1854, at the State Fair in Springfield, Illinois, he was dressed so badly that his wife was ashamed of him; yet he made there the first great speech of his life, a speech that started him on a career that gave him a place among the immortals.

Errors in grammar won't kill a speech: I have heard thrilling talks that were sprinkled with errors in grammar.

Lack of education won't kill a talk: One of my closest friends, Frank Bettger, a man who never finished grade school, has been paid two thousand dollars a week to speak in public.

No, faults won't kill a speech; but a lack of virtues will.

To Stir Your Audience, Get Stirred Yourself

So tonight, forget about the underbrush of public speaking and look up through the tree tops at the stars. Concentrate tonight on the one big essential: producing a mental and emotional effect on your listeners. How can you do that? By first producing it inside yourself.

157

For example, around the turn of the century, a magazine publisher got wrought up because people had so little loyalty, enthusiasm and initiative. He had been troubled about this for twenty years. One day he poured out his feelings in a short article that later appeared in one of his magazines. That article, dashed off at white heat, created a sensation. Orders for copies of it came pouring in from all over America. A hundred copies! A thousand! Ten thousand! The New York Central Railroad gave a copy to every one of its employees. So did hundreds of other corporations. The Russian army gave a copy to every Russian soldier in the Russo-Japanese War of 1904-05. And so did the Japanese army. Before the author died, forty million copies of that article had been reprinted —a world's record. I am talking about "A Message to Garcia," by Elbert Hubbard. (By the way, if you would like to read it, you will find it on Pages 553 to 557 of *Public Speaking and Influencing Men In Business.*)

Speak on a Subject You Feel Deeply

Tonight I want you to do what Elbert Hubbard did. I want you to speak out of the depths of your heart and feelings and convictions. Select a subject that you have been preparing to talk about for ten or twenty years. Speak on something you have earned the right to talk about.

If you do that, you can forget all about gestures because your gestures will make themselves. If you do that, you can forget audience contact because you couldn't look away from your audience if you tried. If you do that, you can forget all about animation because your animation will come boiling up like a geyser.

158

I once asked Vash Young how he wrote his inspiring book, *A Fortune to Share*. He replied, "I didn't write it. It *exploded* from me."

That is what I want your talk to do tonight: *explode* from you.

Pick a Subject That Will "Explode"!

A subject? You will have to roll your own. I don't know what experiences and ideas have struck you with the impact of a Kansas cyclone, *but you do*. Here are a few suggestions that may help:

1. The strongest conviction of my life.
2. My most moving experience.
3. My biggest regret.
4. The most important lesson I have learned.
5. My biggest battle with myself.
6. My greatest handicap.
7. What my children have taught me.
8. What I want most to give my children.
9. My secret ambition.
10. My greatest musical experience.
11. The person who has influenced me most.
12. The book that has influenced me most.
13. My favorite motto—and what it has meant to me.
14. The mental and emotional impact that this course has had on me.
15. The kind of job I'd like to have.
16. The biggest surprise of my life.
17. The worst headache I ever had in business.
18. What I dislike about my in-laws.
19. The biggest fool thing I ever did.

159

These Rules Will Help You Make a Good Talk

Here are three sound suggestions for your talk to-night:

1. Pick a simple subject—something you can handle adequately in two minutes. Don't talk about universal peace or how to stop all crime. You just can't cover such subjects in two minutes. The simpler and more homespun your subject, the better your speech.

2. Be absolutely sure you have one good, interesting example.

NOTE—Your instructor has been told not to accept your talk tonight *unless it contains an example.*

3. Use a *ho hum* that follows the rules in the booklet, *How to Put Magic in the Magic Formula.*

In this part of the session, the best speech and most improvement pencils will be awarded.

Talks, Prizes and Reading Assignment
Session Number Sixteen

Talks:

> 6:00 to 8:00 p.m. session—2 minutes—Talk for "What I Got Out of the Course" championship.
>
> 8:00 to 10:40 p.m. session—2 minutes—Speak on a subject you feel deeply.

Prizes:

> 6:00 to 8:00 p.m. session—Championship pencil for the student who makes the best talk on "What I Got Out of the Course."
>
> 8:00 to 10:40 p.m. session—Best speech and most improvement pencils.

Reading Assignment:

> No reading assignment.

160

COMMENCEMENT EXERCISES

Date...

Time...

Place...

The Commencement Exercises

Your class usually meets with other classes for your commencement exercises.

Informal dress! Unique program! Interesting talks! Awards! Presentation of diplomas! Bring as many guests, male or female, as you care to finance.

In most cities, speaking contests are held, in which the class representatives compete for the championships.

A commencement address by an outstanding business man, a leading educator, or a representative of Dale Carnegie may be the cap-stone of this commencement evening. Or, perhaps, the sponsor in your city may prefer to have more student speeches—perhaps brief talks by every member of every class.

The time and place of the commencement exercises will be decided by the sponsor. The exercises will probably not be held on one of the nights your class regularly meets.

The commencement programs can be highly beneficial and inspiring to you. You can have fun and you can bring your friends to enjoy the evening with you. Be sure to be on hand to give the representatives from your class—and you may be one of them—your wholehearted and enthusiastic support.

161

A Message from Dale Carnegie

You have gained in the last few months a sound foundation in effective speaking, personality development and the art of winning friends and influencing people. You have developed habits that will help you to get along better with other people, win more friends, speak with ease, confidence, poise and effectiveness in business and social interviews and before groups.

We urge that you continue to grow by the constant practice of the skills you have gained and the habits you have formed, so that you may attain a more successful, happier and fuller life.

James Allen wrote in *As a Man Thinketh:* "In all human affairs there are efforts and there are results, and the strength of the efforts is the measure of the result."

We hope that you will some day look back upon this training as one of the milestones of your career.

—DALE CARNEGIE

RULES FROM "HOW TO WIN FRIENDS AND INFLUENCE PEOPLE"

Fundamental Techniques in Handling People

1. Don't criticize, condemn or complain.
2. Give honest, sincere appreciation.
3. Arouse in the other person an eager want.

Six Ways to Make People Like You

1. Become genuinely interested in other people.
2. Smile.
3. Remember that a man's name is to him the sweetest and most important sound in the English language.
4. Be a good listener. Encourage others to talk about themselves.
5. Talk in terms of the other man's interests.
6. Make the other person feel important—and do it *sincerely*.

Twelve Ways to Win People to Your Way of Thinking

1. The only way to get the best of an argument is to avoid it.
2. Show respect for the other man's opinion. Never tell a man he is wrong.
3. If you are wrong, admit it quickly and emphatically.
4. Begin in a friendly way.

163

5. Get the other person saying, "yes, yes" immediately.

6. Let the other man do a great deal of the talking.

7. Let the other man feel that the idea is his.

8. Try honestly to see things from the other person's point of view.

9. Be sympathetic with the other person's ideas and desires.

10. Appeal to the nobler motives.

11. Dramatize your ideas.

12. Throw down a challenge.

Nine Ways to Change People Without Giving Offense or Arousing Resentment

1. Begin with praise and honest appreciation.

2. Call attention to people's mistakes indirectly.

3. Talk about your own mistakes before criticizing the other person.

4. Ask questions instead of giving direct orders.

5. Let the other man save his face.

6. Praise the slightest improvement and praise every improvement. Be hearty in your approbation and lavish in your praise.

7. Give the other person a fine reputation to live up to.

8. Use encouragement. Make the fault seem easy to correct.

9. Make the other person happy about doing the thing you suggest.

Seven Rules for Making Your Home Life Happier

1. Don't nag.
2. Don't try to make your partner over.
3. Don't criticize.
4. Give honest appreciation.
5. Pay little attentions.
6. Be courteous.
7. Read a good book on the sexual side of marriage.

WHO WON THE PRIZES

Session	Best Speech	Most Improvement	Special Award

Book Winners:

Lincoln the Unknown	Getting the Most Out of Life	Biographical Roundup

Champions:

Impromptu Speech

Prepared Speech

"What I Got Out of the Course" Speech

CLASS ROLL

Class No. . . . .

NAME	NICKNAME

CLASS ROLL

Class No. . . . .

NAME	NICKNAME

CLASS ROLL

Class No. . . . .

NAME	NICKNAME

MEMORANDUM

Recommended Readings

• Siddhartha by Hermann Hesse

•The Anatomy of Success, Nicolas Darvas

• The Dale Carnegie Course on Effective Speaking, Personality Development, and the Art of How to Win Friends & Influence People, Dale Carnegie

• The Law of Success In Sixteen Lessons by Napoleon Hill (Complete, Unabridged), Napoleon Hill

• It Works, R. H. Jarrett,

• The Art of Public Speaking (Audiobook), Dale Carnegie,

• The Success System That Never Fails (Audio Book), W. Clement Stone,

Printed in the USA
CPSIA information can be obtained
at www.ICGtesting.com
LVHW041934100424
776966LV00003B/435